To the beautiful woman who inspired me to live my DREAM. Thank you so much WENDY WILLIAMS.

The 9 Power Principles for Change

autographed to empower you

to live, dream, and succeed

Azuka Zuke Obi

Keep inspiring Humanity.

AZUKA.

5/4/2015

THE 9

POWER

PRINCIPLES FOR

CHANGE

A Motivational Guide to Excellence

AZUKA ZUKE OBI

Author of The Power to Excel

THE 9

POWER

PRINCIPLES FOR

CHANGE

A Motivational Guide to Excellence

AZUKA ZUKE OBI

Author of The Power to Excel

DEDICATION

To those who read this book yesterday
To those reading this book now
To those who will read this book later today
To those who will read this book tomorrow

To my terrific fans all over the world:
You are awesome people.
I salute your courage for believing in this movement for positive
change.
May the power of change always be with you.

You will excel amazingly in doing things you enjoy. If you're passionate about something, move on and do it graciously with excitement and all your energy.

You'll be surprised by how far you'll go.

–Author Azuka Zuke

APPRECIATION FROM PRESIDENT BARACK OBAMA

The next page contains a letter to me dated July 1, 2013, following the president's receipt of my debut book, The Power to Excel: Reaching for Your Best.

THE WHITE HOUSE
WASHINGTON

We would like to extend our deepest thanks and appreciation for your generous gift.

It is gratifying to know that we have your support. As we work to address the great challenges of our time, we hope you will continue to stay active and involved.

Again, thank you for your kind gift.

Barack Obama   *Michelle Obama*

WWW.WHITEHOUSE.GOV

HONORING JOY OBI EZINNE

This page is created to honor the late Joy Obi Ezinne -good mother, a proud Nigerian woman and West African native born in Eastern Nigeria. She married an amazing man, Mr. Godfery Chukwuka Obi, and with him produced five children, of which I am one. In addition to being my mother, she was my teacher and adviser, imparting both love and discipline into my life. She was cute, educated, kind, and cared tirelessly for people, living with absolute dignity, a giving heart, and humility. She raised me to be strong and demanded that I be humble but confident, and she constantly taught me the principle of determination. She was also an entertainer, and she always offered her opinion on critical matters, which she called plain truth.

Joy, my mother and trusted ally, constantly reminded me of the power of prayer. She was spiritually gifted; she demanded that I always have gratitude and stressed the importance of constantly creating a synthesis. She worked hard in spite of challenges and gave me faith that God is always near. She trained me to be strong and never tolerate intimidation.

She was the connection to my dream, something I will cherish for the rest of my life. She taught me to dream big. She stressed that dreams do come true and that hard work can be rewarding. As a teacher, she knew how to impart knowledge. Because she earned a meager monthly salary, which was oftentimes delayed for months, she supplemented her income with proceeds from non-mechanized farm work, with which I assisted her. Her work ethic was unequalled, and she woke up at five each morning for prayers, a ritual she observed till death. When it was time for work, my mother was simply an enviable workaholic. It was her way of life and the only way to break even, a principle that formed the bedrock of my life's foundation. I learned to never settle for mediocrity and that failure was not an option. When I did fail, she taught me to learn a lesson and then bounce back. I copied her work ethic verbatim. She infused the I-can-do-it attitude in me, demanding that I constantly create opportunities and strive for excellence.

My parents never had the income level of millionaires, but I had the golden opportunity to see successful people as we moved for years before settling in the village. Mum always told me that if I admired those successful people, I should act successful; I would thus create a mental image of success and quadruple my chances of becoming one. She ordered me to follow my dream as if my life depended on it. My mother was a sharp dresser, and she told me to be conscious of personal image. Her shoes always shone like sunlight. Her attire mimicked that of successful Hollywood stars even though she never flew or left the shores of Africa. She only saw them on pages of magazines but used them to present a successful image of herself. And she constantly reminded me to dress well to sharpen my poise.

She was a woman of substance, the epitome of wisdom, a rare gem, a shining example of motherhood, and above all one of the greatest teachers. I totally connected with her principles. I feel blessed for having had the opportunity to spend time with her in her last days on earth before she passed on in June 2004 as I vacationed in Nigeria, West Africa. The memory of that time still powers me today. I will continue to remember you, Mum, for your outstanding qualities and exemplary Christian life, and I still love you for influencing my life in amazing ways. You taught me well. I am glad I copied your principles hook, line, and sinker.

Mama, this book is one of the by-products of your teachings, a movement you initiated.

I give thanks every day for all the sacrifices you made while here.
I bless you for blessing me.
The Lord keep you safe.

HOW TO USE THIS BOOK

First read this affirmation wholeheartedly every morning.

Everything in my life is what I think. I understand the importance of keeping a positive attitude as a force in recreating my life. Every good thing in the universe is flowing into my life now. I have no option but to utilize these resources in transforming my life. I know that I may not reach every nook and cranny of the world, but I can contribute something to make an impact. I believe that if I share the blessings from this book with just one person, I will have initiated a chain reaction that can bless people worldwide, including me. I am making progress in my life. I am supercharged. I am ignited. I am focused. I am creating success.

Now, read the book. After the first reading, think through the major points. Read it a second time, slowly, with emphasis on practicing the tips, underlining statements that strike your attention, and declaring aloud the power corner at the end of each chapter. Over time these declarations will become part and parcel of you as you practice the nine power principles for change to create success in your life.

DIVINE CHANGE

This is the beginning of amazing things in your life. Get ready for a divine change as you tune your frequency to a steady flow of light and total transformation.

In this self-development book, you will discover positive energy:

- *motivation to work on personal goals*
- *drive to make serious positive changes*
- *the power of gratitude*
- *encouragement to navigate life*
- *empowerment to face any challenge*

In addition, you will learn the following:

- *how to draw inspiration from innate resources*
- *how to ignite the power of determination*
- *how the power of giving can transform your life*
- *how to put your faith into action*

ACKNOWLEDGMENTS

As a published author, I have been stretched immensely in various areas of personal growth. My life has moved in a positive direction. I have been singled out and honored in various ways based on the things I have created. I travel widely, honored with several public appearances and have been asked to speak to empower, to inspire, and to motivate others.

I know these achievements were made possible by hard work, determination, faith, and, above all, God's touch. I thank him for protecting me since my birth and for presenting me with golden opportunities. God has been so good to me, holding me in his hands and monitoring every move I make. Whenever I miss my exit, like a GPS he always recalculates to put me back on track. When I think back on all the chances and the various events that have transformed me, I feel grateful because of the presence of his mighty hands in them. These things didn't just happen. He carefully orchestrated them. For these and more to come, I unleash unlimited salutes to God.

I also attribute my blessings to the various people that he placed in my path as I worked on this book. They motivated me when I felt like quitting and assisted in various ways to make this project a huge success. When I reflect on this publishing journey, I feel joyful because they played their roles well in bringing this book into the households of people worldwide. They are reliable and generous and brought out the best in themselves. Their untiring effort provided the instrumental boost that led to the production of this beautiful book.

I sincerely appreciate my family for its support, especially my father, Godfrey Chukwuka Obi, who brought me into this world and taught me how to be a man. Thank you, Dad.

I salute Esther Chioma. Your unshakable faith in me throughout the time I wrote this book was awesome. You catalyzed my dream seed, reignited my intensity every day, and kept me on schedule till I published. You sparked my creativity, rattled my imagination, and backed me with prayers to unlock the puzzles I faced. You're my special adviser, a living example of good energy, and I respect your courage. Thank you so much.

I salute Princess Stella Nkechi Oli for her faith in me. You did things that had a positive impact on my life, constantly interceding in my behalf. Tapping into your spiritual connections was something significant, an experience I will cherish the rest of my life. You represent generosity. You're an invaluable asset and a living example of integrity.

Mayor Jamel C. Holley supported me in a big way as I navigated the hurdles of publishing. Jamel is a powerful young man, a motivator who is always devoting his time to support great causes. I have been honored with your drive.

I thank Gaines Hill, my senior publishing consultant at Amazon. You patiently guided me through the publishing process, believed so much in this project, and told me, "I like the book title. It is powerful." Those words kept me motivated. I bless your positive attitude.

Special thanks to Professor Terry Benjamin for his constructive but honest advice during the production of this book. You encouraged my rapid growth by embracing me in your circle and told me, "You haven't seen anything." Those are rare, powerful words. You are a living example of a free spirit.

My sincere gratitude to Emmanuel Ofili, my mentor, for his guidance and encouragement. You're resourceful, and I applaud your brotherhood. Thank you for your loyalty and dedication. You are a living human force.

I humbly salute Dr. Kevin West for doing so many positive things as I penned this book. Those beautiful comments you made and the things you did were instrumental in my drive to succeed. They energized me, motivated me to work harder, and ignited the positive vibrations in me. You are a good man, humble, ubiquitous with your blessings, and a living example of positive support.

I am deeply grateful to the Principal, Vice-Principal, Teachers, Academic and Non-academic staff and the very respectful students of Leonard V. Moore Middle School, Roselle, New Jersey for their friendship and partnership. These amazing people always welcome me to their school with good energy and inspire me to reach greater heights as I champion this movement for positive change. Their students are just amazing and I am deeply grateful for their respect. Their untiring supports and inspiration helped in making this book a great success story.

I thank Andrea Holmes Thompkins, president and CEO of ACE Media Corporation in New York, for the surprises she sent my way as I wrote this book. You connected big-time with this movement and believed so much in what I wanted to achieve. Andrea, you are humble, unique, elegant, resourceful, generous, and a blessing to humanity. You are loaded with good energy and a practical example of female power. I thank God for putting you in my path.

I salute Dominique, my former photo specialist at Target in Linden, New Jersey. You took different skillful shots of me with laughter and humor, making sure you got a perfect pose for the author photo. You even paid half of the bill and said, "I want to sow a seed to invest in your noble cause." That was amazing. I am still humbled by that noble act of giving. Thank you, Dominique.

A big thank you to Mary A. Rega for playing a great role in seeing to the success of this book. You motivated me to writing tirelessly till I published. You are very humane, and strongly believe in what I wanted to achieve. The exposure you gave this book and my other books will always be appreciated. You are a living example of a great publicity associate.

To Rev. James E. Moore Snr; Yvonne Ashby, Rev. Barbara D. Turner , Carol Stewart, Renee Brown, Tochukwu Oscar Udeh, Kathy Lloyd, David T. Holmes III, and CJ Arditi. These people constantly inspire me by injecting amazing faith in me to lift myself to greater levels of achievement so that I can fulfill my dreams of touching many lives with my writing gifts. Thank you so much for the good energy you bring with you.

Sincere thanks to my Editor, Martha for your thorough and comprehensive editing of my manuscript. Your professional guidance and constructive recommendations formed the bedrock upon which the beauty and readability of this book are anchored. Your editorial skills are terrific and are highly appreciated. Thank you so much.

I honor Adam Dill Reid for his artistic originality. Adam is the architect of the graphics design of this book cover and backed me up big-time. Adam is a living example of a great graphic artist. Thank you, Adam, for your timely response when your skills were needed most.

I thank all who have bought books, posted reviews, honored my appearances or attended my motivational speaking events, book discussions, and signings and made positive comments. You are a great force, and it's very gratifying to know that you believe in this movement.

Finally, I humbly salute my content media coordinator and my project coordination and development team for making time for me and offering up their patience and professional skills to transform my manuscript into an edificial masterpiece at Amazon.com. You all are awesome people, a great team and it is very gratifying working with you.

CONTENTS

ACKNOWLEDGMENTS..*XXIII*

PREFACE..*XXXI*

INTRODUCTION..*XLV*

THE POWER OF PRAYER: A MOVING FORCE 1

THE POWER OF DETERMINATION: A KEY TO SUCCESS...............11

THE POWER OF CONNECTIONS: NETWORKING TO EXPAND...............27

THE POWER OF MEDITATION: SOOTHING THE SOUL...............39

THE POWER OF EXERCISE AND GOOD FOOD: FOR
OPTIMAL HEALTH..47

THE POWER OF GIVING: OPENING DOORS FOR ABUNDANCE..........57

THE POWER OF HUMILITY: A KEY TO SUCCESS...............................65

THE POWER OF LOVE: IT CONQUERS EVERYTHING 73

THE POWER OF GRATITUDE: MAGNIFYING OUR BLESSINGS...................81

YOU HAVE HEALING POWERS TO CREATE CHANGE 93

FORTY-FIVE POWER QUOTES FOR POSITIVE CHANGE................97

PREFACE

Growing up under the guidance of very strict parents in a remote village in Eastern Nigeria, West Africa, I hit many roadblocks. At one point, I thought the whole world was crashing down on me. However, having come from a tough background and being a by-product of my disciplinarian parents, I have always been guided by the principles of determination and hard work, encouraged by prayers and the belief that I could always overcome tribulations. These were the principles my life revolved around, a force reinforced regularly by my late mother. The knowledge I received growing up widened my perspective and sharpened my desire for improvement and my drive to expand my capacities for living a successful life. Coming from a deprived background defined by rectitude, discipline, limited funds and resources, I had no option but to live within my means while hoping for better days. I tackled challenges with determination and a flow of constant gratitude for life—for food on the table, clothing, the air I breathed, the roof over my head, my dreams, my health, and the opportunities to explore the day's blessings with hope and faith in the almighty God.

A very strong belief in my local culture played a great role in my upbringing, and I am still a pure product of that strict culture. Every parent in the village became my parent and was to be respected and obeyed. Although I walked miles to school on foot, often with no pocket money for snacks, I always retained a feeling of gratitude. My late mother always advocated the importance of keeping a positive attitude even when things seemed tough. My father could not afford a car, a luxury meant for the rich and well-to-do in our society, a dream that seemed impossible to the common villager. We were abundantly content, so it never mattered if we had a car or not, nor was it an issue if I walked to school year-round. Mum was always around; she monitored every move I made, offered serious reprimand when the situation called for such, and always recalculated my steps to put me back on track. She kept an eagle eye on me. We were defined by discipline, love, and a spirit of togetherness, and communal living was the order of the day. My mother constantly advised me to live my dream and follow my passion. She constantly stressed the importance of trusting my instincts. I am blessed today because of those principles she strongly emphasized.

After school and homework completion, I went out with friends to assist other children in the neighborhood to complete their chores. Then we'd have fun and immerse ourselves in the beautiful games of village life. Saturdays were a time to go food shopping at the local market or to complete farm work. I accompanied Mum to the farms to till the soil and cultivate all kinds of vegetables and farm products. We planted yams, palm fruits, and bananas, which I would cut down upon maturity and carry on my head to the family house. We worked tirelessly in our farms from morning till midafternoon, taking breaks to refuel with food we had cooked with a makeshift fireplace right there in the farm. We cooked with caution to avoid starting a wildfire. It was risky but so much fun. On some weekends my friends and I would travel for miles on foot to fetch firewood. We'd carry it on our heads, stopping now and then for rest and water on the long journey back home. We did not grow up with gas cookers, so we utilized the thermal energy generated by the firewood for cooking. I would rearrange some of the firewood for onward dispatch to the local market to be sold to make some change to beef up the standards in my wallet. Mum supplemented whenever she could.

We played soccer as well. Although we played at a very local level, we displayed skill. Nothing could keep us from playing: we lived life to its fullest, enjoying and appreciating every single day. Since we could not afford real soccer balls due to limited resources, we played with any round object we could find, including oranges. Finding a used plastic ball on the road was a fantastic bonus, and we would play all day with excitement and gratitude to God for his miracles. We played hide-and-seek as the moon came out at night within the confines of our family house and shared moonlit stories coordinated by team leaders. After an exhausting evening of games, my mother would remind me to say a prayer before going to bed, which later became part and parcel of my life and has blessed me real good. To this day I honor God and salute the universe for its wonders.

Festivities like Christmas were cause for celebration. We deeply believed in the birth of Jesus, for Christianity ran in our bloodline. We would kick off Christmas with a church service, having walked miles to reach the place of worship. In the afternoon, after lunch, we would dress up in our brand-new clothes and visit different families to celebrate in grand style. We were never confined to our family home. We went everywhere, usually ending up at the market square to watch a display of different masquerades from various communities around town. It mimicked some sort of Caribbean carnival.

New Year's came with its own fun-filled excitement as we paraded through the villages, brandishing our new clothes specifically designed for the occasion, having prayed all night at church to usher in the New Year. Although funds were limited, we never were denied the free rights of happiness, love, oneness, and free celebration.

Despite all the challenges that presented their ugly heads during my childhood, I never deviated from my focus or went off track from what

I wanted to achieve. I embraced positivity and followed my instincts, asking God to direct my path at all times and to constantly place me in favorable locations. He perfectly orchestrated my actions, and I am deeply grateful for his blessings.

High school was tough—years of receiving lectures from unhappy and underpaid teachers who could whip students recklessly for the slightest mistake. Having freedom of speech but the wrong answer came with serious consequences, including but not limited to corporal punishment. The code of conduct was simply discipline. I still recall my primary five school teacher taking me home with her—with my mother's approval—because I hadn't done my homework. I completed the homework with tears in my eyes to secure my release. That was the society where I grew up, in a remote village called Isu, in Eastern Nigeria, West Africa.

In high school, we had one old van minimally used to transport the soccer team to games and transport students to represent the school in science quiz competitions. I had the opportunity to ride in the van, regularly being in the first eleven of our school's soccer team. Although I never played up to Pele's standards, I was very good. The knowledge and skills I acquired in high school came in handy: I graduated with flying colors and even won a couple of laurels during the annual graduation ceremony, including the award for best-behaved student. It took me two years of intense study to pass the entrance examination into the university, where the years were marred by academic strikes and stay-at-home to protest the low wages paid to our university professors.

Graduating from the University of Nigeria, a herculean task, was made possible by grants, scholarships, and personal donations from kind-hearted individuals who knew the challenges presented by the Nigerian academic system and were willing to offer their support. It was tough to succeed in an academic system characterized by professors protesting poor working conditions or nonpayment of their meager monthly salaries. Withholding the teachers' paychecks was a normal thing, though something unheard of in the Western world.

Students had their own challenges. We oftentimes stayed on campus without adequate water supply. When water was available, it was often not clean enough for human consumption. Food resources were limited, too. Morale was very low. On campus we referred to money as morale. On very rough days, we had to travel miles to fetch water or wash our clothes at the local rivers surrounding the campus, something we enjoyed doing because we had no choice.

Academic studies brought additional challenges. Often we studied with candles and lanterns. We grew accustomed to the epileptic supply of electricity. We would go without power for days, celebrating excitedly whenever it was restored. Communication on campus was limited to personal, unannounced visits. No one could afford a cell phone on campus, not even the professors. A cell phone was a luxury meant only for the rich—the big boys and the glamour girls. A few outdated computers were displayed in the campus libraries, and we lined up just to have a feel of their operations.

The years I spent in the university were some of the toughest of my life, and my memory of that time continues to empower me today. Despite the challenges, I had a few moments that blew my mind with joy. The most striking was having my article read as commentary after the news on Radio Nigeria, the national network news that almost every adult in Nigeria tuned in to. The article was on violence in soccer; the radio station, having earlier published on a weekend soccer tabloid, found it appealing. Hearing my name on national radio was empowering and humbling, a memory that will live in me even when I die.

Immigrating to America upon graduation from the university was a big dream that masked obstacles and created a massive avenue for personal growth. It also created a cascade of forums for creating greater opportunities while expanding my drive to pursue the American dream. On that maiden flight of my life, we flew over the Atlantic Ocean through Holland. Landing at Schiphol Airport in Amsterdam after a six-hour flight from Lagos, Nigeria, was fascinating. As the jumbo jet rolled in the drizzling rain for a connecting flight to the United States, I kept my eyes fixed on the architectural beauty of the structural edifices at the airport, a memory I still feel today.

The connecting flight was smooth at takeoff. We hit some turbulence midair, but the excitement of flying for the first time masked my fear as I looked forward to landing in America. Sandwiched between two beautiful white women, I did not know what food to ask for from the hostesses; I simply nodded "yes" to every in-flight food offered.

Eight hours later we flew into the American airspace through New York City. Looking through the tiny window of the aircraft, I saw the Statue of Liberty standing tall with dignity and witnessed from midair a view of one of the world's most iconic skylines—what until then I had only heard about on radio broadcasts or seen in pictures in newspapers or on television back home in West Africa. I got goose bumps: joy filled my heart, and tears ran down my cheek. Nothing is as exciting as landing at a city you are visiting for the very first time. In no time the pilot announced our landing at Liberty Airport. It was a sweet sound. Liberty to express myself, liberty to work with dignity, to operate with freedom, to excel and create. And so I started my journey in America.

When I recall the challenges I faced at the University of Nigeria, including an inability to rent a suit for my graduation or afford a computer (I never really used one until I immigrated to America), I feel very grateful for the goodness of God in my life. My first computer was a desktop model, a gift from a church member who was relocating to Texas and needed to give away some things. It was a fifteen-inch white computer with a posterior projecting tube, and it was really exciting. I was full of joy and gratitude.

Immigrating to the United States showed God's power in action. While at the university, I assured myself that I would one day live in the United States. I never for one day doubted my feelings, a sensation that constantly boiled inside. I only waited for the opportunity. I visualized myself living in America; I talked, acted, and dressed American; I memorized all fifty states and recited them like a poem. Everything about me was American even though I'd never even flown to the next city in Nigeria. I was blessed with some strange force running inside my system—faith. And that faith has carried me through every challenge I have encountered.

Immigrating to the United States with twenty-five dollars in my wallet came with its own blessings and challenges. I first worked at Wendy's restaurant, at times fetching things from the cold room, and I worked as a library custodian, putting outdated books at the curb and oftentimes asking people if it was OK to take out their garbage. I did a couple of other jobs and over time progressed to office work and career work. Eventually I became an author, a publisher, and a motivational speaker, and the rest is history. God has been so good to me, and I owe him my gratitude forever.

I strongly believe that every human has the potential to improve his or her life and bounce back from the lowest level to the extraordinary. Oftentimes we are limited by ourselves and our beliefs and subject ourselves to irrational fears. This is why many people who want to be successful aren't. Poisoned by their own fear, they become paranoid; they suffer paralysis and stop living their dream. You don't have to be a super-star to do great things. No one is born a success. Success is a function of dedication, hard work, determination, persistence, desire for growth, and, above all, God's mighty touch. If you do something with all your energy and focus, you'll see positive results.

Before I published my first book, The Power to Excel, on Amazon, I knew I would work hard to see results. I made sure I wrote daily. When I couldn't write, I edited to stay engaged but never deviated from focus. I knew I was creating something that would change people's lives. Upon publishing, I persistently promoted my book, did book signings, and gave pro bono speeches in schools and communities to give back. I never left a speech without handing out my business card with instructions on how to purchase the book. I applied high intense energy and developed an evangelical attitude in marketing my book. I sent out autographed copies to randomly selected people and received positive feedback. The first was a reply from the Nigerian ambassador to New York, assuring me that my book would form part of the reference material in their library. President Obama received a copy at the White House and sent a thank-you letter for my autographed book. I was elated to receive a letter from a sitting president of the United States. I felt great as I con-tinued to promote my book, and the results have been astonishing.

Do you persist when taking actions, or do you chicken out when you hit a roadblock? One grave mistake people make is thinking that successful people are special, highly educated, or just unique. No one is more unique or talented than anyone else. Everybody is talented, includ-ing you. You're a brand. Now, place your right hand on your head and declare aloud, "I am unique, I am a brand, I am talented, I am endowed with what it takes to succeed."

When you constantly but humbly affirm your resourcefulness, even when around people, you send divine messages to the universe about your uniqueness and specialness. Successful people are those who choose to work hard to develop a brand, decide to make a change, and believe in their dreams. They take calculated risks and never quit. How can you develop this mind-set? Start by taking up simple tasks. Then set a target on what is to be achieved, and work toward it with a deep sense of commitment and nothing but victory in mind. Resolve today to push without fear. If you bury intimidation and work consistently, over time you'll see results.

What are your fears today? What will they be tomorrow, next month, or next year? What about in five or ten years from now? Whatever they are, stop those fears—now. How? Write your fears down carefully on a piece of paper, and write something positive to counter each fear on the opposite side of the paper. Continue working diligently until you eliminate the fears. Fear is simply rubbish—it's useless—so don't let these surmountable insecurities stop you from moving forward. I empower you today to stop fear: take the bull by the horns like an African lion, and live the dream that God deposited in you. Banish fear, flush out paralysis, think tough, and take bold actions, irrespective of the accompanying sacrifices. No matter your age or circumstances, you can still do great things. No matter how miserable you look today, you can still bounce back because God understands your challenges and is working behind the scenes in your behalf even without your knowledge.

Consider the following, from Exodus 3:7: "Then the Lord said, 'I have observed the misery of my people who are in Egypt; I have heard their cry on account of their taskmasters. Indeed, I know their sufferings.'" He knows what you're going through. So relax, work with faith, and he'll see you through. Then take on another task, visualize it as completed, work, and move on to a more cumbersome project. It won't be long before you see results. Success is a relative term. Only you can define it. Sometimes you need to take a little risk, and if you don't quit, you'll surely shine. When people ask me how I became a published author despite distractions, I tell them this: I never gave up. I did not quit, even when I felt like it. I believed and worked very hard—as if my life depended on it. I trusted God, and it worked.

Several years of procrastination passed before I actually wrote my first book. Those were the most wasted years of my life. Procrastination is a dream killer, and it almost shattered my dream. I thank God it didn't. I knew I could produce good stuff, but I never really got my act together to create anything. But when I made the first move, defied all obstacles, overcame tribulations, and blocked all forms of distracting energy, the results came. It worked for me, and it can work for you if only you believe. If you're not doing something new every quarter of the year and taking calculated risks to improve your life, you are procrastinating and wasting your internal God-given energies. You have to constantly create opportunities. If you're not creating or grabbing opportunities, you're losing great possibilities to make a big change in your life.

The humans that first went to space may not have succeeded if they'd been fearful or listened to criticism. They didn't just wake up one day and fly. They prepared tirelessly for years and built courage, confidence, internal energy, and emotional and physical strength prior to making that move. Despite their awareness of the risks involved, they acted. Why did they succeed? Because they were determined and mentally prepared. No doubt there were lapses, but they never stopped dreaming. It was in their mind-set; they believed in the possibilities and made history. Understand one thing: every great achievement first passed through errors and failures. Thomas Alva Edison, a disciple of the great physicists, performed hundreds of unrelenting trials to create the first practical electric light bulb in Roselle, New Jersey, in 1883. That is persistence.

The scriptures offer another good example of the power of persistence. The prophet Elisha told Nahman to go dip himself seven times in the River Jordan to be healed of leprosy. From the first to the sixth dip, nothing happened. Yet Nahman did not give up, and on the seventh, he was healed. Miracles sometimes follow false starts, so you must keep trying. Believe that your miracle is around the next corner, the catalyst to ignite that green light that initiates the chain reaction for positive change.

In the creative world of human achievement, whether in psychology or engineering, philosophy or mountaineering, you'll discover that most successes are preceded by trials. This means you have no prior knowledge of the workability or outcome of your actions. So persistently work hard, build an adaptive immunity to change, stay faithful, step up your momentum with a positive mind-set, and be ready to launch yourself to the next level. To create change, you must feel and embrace change.

As an author, I salute God for the various metamorphoses he has introduced into my life. I have never failed to express my feelings of unalloyed gratitude for the various ways he has rearranged, restructured, and repackaged my life. I thank God for change because change has remodeled me and has transformed my life into a global phenomenon.

You, too, can create change if you're willing to tear up that soil, turn up heavy stones, sweat, and invest time and energy to nurture your dreams while taking calculated risks. If you do, in due time, you'll harvest cheerfully. Psalm 126:6 reassures us of this eventual positive outcome: "Those who wept as they went out carrying the seeds will come back singing for joy, as they bring in the harvest."

In human creativity, constant verbalization of affirmations works. So confirm, affirm, and reaffirm your dreams. There is power in your words that is waiting to come out. Pronounce them wholeheartedly, for they can mend, fix, and transform your life. The frequently neglected but most effective words are the unspoken ones, but all words have energy, whether you are speaking to yourself or complementing or applauding others. Your thoughts have no potency unless you verbalize them. Put into words, your affirmations travel and align with the creative magnetic forces of the universe to produce a carbon-copy manifestation of what you speak. If you speak negative words, be ready for negativity to come to you. If you speak positively, be ready for the accompanying blessings.

How does this work? When you believe what you say with all your heart, your words create a solid foundation. This means that you have to constantly speak and act positively in the direction of your dream in order to see desired results. You must always evolve by saying positive things to yourself by making your declarations known to the universe and by so doing you create ahead of time exactly what you intend to achieve. Resolve today to speak words of faith in your life and to others who need them. It's OK to be effusive with your positive words; be generous with them. Such generosity blesses people, and it blesses you. As difficult as attaining your goal seems, you can make it only if you're willing to speak, affirm, believe, and try committing to your goals, blessing others both verbally and practically while working toward success.

A large part of success is loving what you do. This creates a feeling of joy and makes you more genuine and accomplished. When I published my maiden book, The Power to Excel, a self-help book, on Amazon, Kindle, Audible, BN.com, and iTunes, I knew it would generate passive income, and it sure did. That's not all. I gave a few copies to people I believed the book would empower. I gave out random copies based on my instincts to students, seniors, and those that my giving spirit connected with. I gave copies every month to those who most needed the book and the inspiration it carried, and that felt great. I gave out the Kindle version in free promotions at Amazon.com, and I was shocked by the number of downloads of my book worldwide including in India, Spain, Canada, Brazil, Italy, the United Kingdom, Australia, and Denmark, to mention but a few. My fan base blew up worldwide. Reviews trickled in, and my Amazon ranking improved. That put a smile on my face.

Love what you do. Give—give with passion and humility. When you do what you love with passion and give with love, you create a mental picture of passion; you draw attention and attract support to champion your cause. Your gifts have energy. Those you give to will remember you and feel the energy in your gift. Give something today, and watch how you feel. When you give, you transmit giving energy, you feel good, and the recipients feel good. There is a difference between people who do what they love and those who don't. When you love what you do, you emit passion and discover more. And regular practice with passion makes you an expert.

Oftentimes we give and expect immediate rewards. That's the wrong approach. You may not see immediate paybacks for your acts of kindness. When that happens, be patient. Continue to bless people, for God may be putting you through a process of reconstruction. Life may present challenges and friends may become unreliable, but if you remain generous and patient, it won't be long before you see generosity emerge in your life. If you're patient in the midst of storm, you'll feel better and stronger soon afterward. In winter the trees widen, lose their leaves, and seem lifeless, standing like artificial poles. But as springtime approaches, the leaves flourish again with beautiful flowers. The lesson here is this: when things aren't going well, be calm. Believe that God is working behind the scenes, refining you.

INTRODUCTION

Though I authored The Power to Excel: Reaching for Your Best, I resolved to keep writing to the best of my ability to create avenues through which people who read my books could make positive changes to their lives with the ultimate goal of achieving life-changing success. I have always used the power of simplicity to get my message across. This book outlines some tips you can apply for a total turnaround and refurbishing of your life. These tips draw on your natural, innate resources and work in alliance with the universe. These powers are inside you, but you must be willing to apply them to ignite the attractive benefits.

When I briefly studied the law of attraction for the first time, I was shocked by its power and amazed by its wonders. I began practicing the law, and as I immersed myself deeper, my life changed. I experienced a solid reconstruction of my personality as I started reaping the abundant benefits. It was my ultimate saving grace, the anointing water that flushed out the impurities in my system, the concrete foundation upon which my new instincts depended. I began to grow more inquisitive; I listened to and learned from people, irrespective of age, religion, status, ethnicity, and social background, and I got very interesting answers. My hunger for knowledge tripled, and I made up my mind to connect fully with the movement. My drive to succeed multiplied intensely because I finally understood how the law worked and how to apply it to my beautiful life. I taught people in my public speaking appearances the new foundation upon which my life was built. Things shifted positively to my advantage in ways that were astonishing and beyond my comprehension. I excelled, achieving things I could never have imagined. I launched into the global limelight. Then it dawned on me: this is a universal law that works for those who believe in it and apply it. It is everywhere, a practical reliable foundation upon which everything stands.

To tap into this foundation, you must be willing to understand its operations. First, monitor your feelings, for these become your thoughts. Then evaluate your thoughts and your belief system, for these become the basis of the actions that inject mechanical force into projects to produce results.

Feel →Think →Act →Believe →Results

For this to work, you must define yourself by knowing exactly what you want to achieve and believing in your capabilities to make things happen. You must trust your abilities to feel, think and get to work before you can see results. You must believe in yourself. Then master your thoughts and take responsibility for your dreams and aspirations. Keep track of your direction, think, plan, believe, and work. Actions create reactions. When you act, you create a chain of events. When I released The Power to Excel on Amazon, I automatically became a published author, motivational speaker, and instant inspiration; I became popular. I spoke at functions, including kids' events about having passion and following their dreams. I released different versions of my book, including an audiobook, and made money from time to time. Do you see the compounding effects of positive actions here?

You, too, can achieve great things if you define yourself, believe in yourself, and work hard. You must be positively oriented, meaning you must free yourself from all forms of negative thinking. Negativity is a bond that attaches you to poverty and then flushes you into disaster.

Stop negativity today, and totally withdraw from its destructive bondage. How?

Follow the steps outlined below to step away from negativity and move forward today:

1. Create positive mental pictures and videos of everything that has happened in your life, both good and bad. Dwell on the good events. You can learn positive things from the bad experiences, but do not dwell on the negative past. Recall every moment that brought good feelings—growing up, going to school, in public, at home—and replay them several times a day in your head. Guess what? These memories will make you smile. This is good for you and your immunity.

2. Next write these events somewhere you can see them daily and recite them aloud with excitement. This generates what I call the physiological effects of positive recitation. These positive events make up your history, and you should be joyful reciting them. Written blessings are better appreciated than mental blessings.

3. Think about a song that makes you sing along whenever it plays. Feel free to dance or nod to the rhythm. Doing so creates joy, a form of positive energy.

As you practice these exercises, you'll feel great; you'll vibrate with an emotional high and limit the chances of thinking useless, nonproductive thoughts. You'll create an exciting atmosphere, which is a proven catalyst for productivity.

You're alive now and reading this book, which means you're already blessed. From birth, your success has been destined. You've been carefully selected to be part of this universal movement. Create a mental image of your usefulness in this world and strive to make an impact while here by living your dreams to the fullest. Every human being is created with unlimited potential from birth, including you. Have you lost your vibe? Or are you firing on all cylinders? Decide today to activate your heroic energy to create a new life.

I want you to do the following exercise. Do it with assurance and belief. Place your right palm on your chest, covering your heart, and loudly declare the following statements:

I have been chosen right from conception.

I was created with unlimited potential.

My heart is beating with positive energy. I can feel the pulsation now.

I am attracting only good things into my life.

I am totally blessed and excited to be where I am right now.

I was created to achieve great things, and I am doing just that.

I have life-changing power deeply rooted inside.

I am destined to succeed in everything I lay my hands on.

I am alive, living my dream, and surrounded by beautiful things.

My whole life is flowing with abundance; all my aspirations are realizable.

My life is full of love, energy, and calm; I am stress-free and moving forward.

The power of God is upon me; I lack nothing, and I am deeply grateful.

Affirm, believe, and recite these words every single day while working harder to actualize your dreams. Declare them with vitality. A human being without vibe is like a work of art without a message. Vitality is the ingredient that adds beauty to life. You're already blessed with supernatural potential for excitement that is just waiting to be ignited. You must now restructure and redirect your intentions and thoughts to amazing and positive stuff. Focusing on negativity inflicts spiritual paralysis. Instead, ignite the positive energy deeply rooted inside you. Understand that your potential is activated further as you grow. You were created to expand, invent, live, enhance, work, love, and enjoy the fruits of your labor to the fullest. You must make a little shift from the usual way of doing things. A little touch of class and deviation from the norm produces unexpected results in your life and when you see results, you must step up your game to the next level.

You were created to dream large. There's nothing wrong with that, and you can never shortchange yourself now. God wants us to dream and live big with humility. Dreaming big is an attribute of his blessings designed for his people, whom he manufactured in his own image. Remember that he is a big God and that you're a chosen one, and I can assure you right now that you'll achieve those dreams if you diligently work on them. Don't stop dreaming. Don't give up. Rather, push harder with determination, vigor, faith, and fluidity. We are meant to be content, but sometimes our plans, calculations, and permutations are totally different from God's. Not reaching your heart's desires as quickly as you want does not mean you have failed. Sometimes God delays you to keep you safe or more focused, to recharge your faith to make you better equipped and ready for the bigger blessings ahead. So when things don't work out fast, just maintain your poise, keep your cool, and be patient.

Patience is very important. It destroys obstacles that ordinarily would have pushed you into dangerous waters. Patience, like determination, is one of the most powerful keys to success. It is a virtue, a powerful skill, an art—not just a flash-in-the-pan phenomenon. Patience is not complacency but a time of waiting, paying attention to your existence, and unfolding a new you. It means silently waiting for God to speak. Impatience drains you, agitates your system, and tires you out. How do you stop impatience? It's simple. Constantly remind yourself to be calm; believing it's a time to redress your wrongs, a transitional phase of your new life, a time of reawakening.

We are meant to do amazing things. We are meant to be loved, enjoy life, sing great songs, dream, believe, travel to different continents, explore opportunities, or even perform on stage irrespective of who is applauding, directing the show, frowning, or cheering us on. Every good thing we're programmed to do is a function of the universal compass and comes with its accompanying rules. When applied the right way with belief, you'll generate success. Even when you're off track, God will redirect you. That's how he works. But you must be willing to play by the rules with faith to reach victory. If you're captaining a team to win a game, all must play hard by the rules. So to achieve, you must play by the rules.

Success occurs when the happiness inherent in hard work flows at its fullest. It is a function of faith, a by-product of incremental but steady positive actions toward desired goals. Success may not make you happy, but happiness generates opportunities for success to find you. Irrespective of your definition of success or your dreams, determination is key. As a child I thought that the only yardstick for measuring success was material effects. But as I grew older, I began to understand that success goes beyond wealth. I began to explore options to create a beautiful life and learned that success is not only the acquisition of wealth but includes little things such as having food on the table, being able to speak in public with confidence, graduating from college, and having children, a job, a loving life, happiness, beautiful relationships, a free spirit, emotional stability, good health, a heart of giving, inner peace, and the ability to see, laugh, and hear when others speak.

Amazing success lies in your confidence, your excitatory laughter, your sense of humor, the people you support, and in whatever you perceive as success. In other words success is relative: it depends on your perception. Only when you begin to see success in everything you do on a daily basis, and not just in the accumulation of wealth, can you understand its true meaning. Success comes with making positive moves by understanding things from a divine perspective. Every human has the capacity for personal growth, but certain things must be in place for this to occur. Understand, we're created by a powerful God who is merciful, reactive to our good thoughts, and willing to help us prosper. But you must be positive. That's when God perceives your dream as something that will benefit his creations and will make sure he perfects it by providing you the resources to actualize it. You must utilize the tools he provides. You must be willing to accept failure when it strikes and make adjustments often. When something does not work as planned, don't stay sad dwelling on the failures; learn lessons from the failures, and then launch another project. There is joy in doing new things.

The stakeholders and super powers in today's technological discoveries were failures at some point. Research a few, and you'll find out. They didn't know the transformative power of their acts. They failed, reinvented, tried new things, invested energy and time, presented their work to God, believed, and took off dreaming and working hard. There is always something to dream of. Dreaming means believing in order to actualize your goals. It works with the principle of the law of attraction. This is a law that works globally and is a way you focus and attract anything you want in your life. A few things I desired would come my way whenever I focused on it, prayed about it, and dreamt about it, a manifestation on my innate powers. It is a way you own, manage and control your thoughts. If you feel, think, dream, believe, and work, you'll sure achieve. Oftentimes people are busy figuring out the operations of this law. That's a waste of time. I tell people to just believe the law works, put it into practice, and watch their lives change.

Growing up, I applied the law of attraction naively. But it worked for me then and is still working. I always knew what I wanted, believed, and got it. I wanted to be the best graduating student in my class in high school. I visualized mounting the stage, my shoulders high, and receiving the prestigious prize during the annual graduation ceremony. I practiced my steps, did mock rehearsals with my mother prompting me, and believed strongly. I held a mental image of the prize I wanted. And when my name was announced, I celebrated. I didn't realize then that I was practicing the law of attraction. All I did was have a laser image of what I wanted and believed in it with faith. And I got it.

The law of attraction is everywhere. It is in your school, in your home, in your car, and in your mind. It is in Africa, Europe, Asia, Oceania, and South America. It is in your school. It is at your mother in-law's house, in the church, the kitchen, the senior citizens' home, and inside the public bus. It is everywhere. It is inside you and is always in motion. You can practice and make it your lifestyle. Have you ever thought of something awhile and then seen it manifest? That is the law of attraction at work. When you have a need, feel it constantly, and magnify that feeling a billion times, channeling it to exactly what you want. The law of attraction works best with hard work, belief, motivation, persistence, consistency, and faith. It worked for me in high school and in immigrating to America, and it continues to work today. Guess what? It'll work for you, too.

Now, I want you to put your attractive force in action. Raise your right hand in the air with all the fingers pointing upward, and make this powerful declaration with faith: I strongly believe in the law of attraction. I am attracting every good thing in my life. I believe with faith in my great future, and I am living large. I am attracting beautiful relationships, a good life, and happiness. I am attracting powerful and useful people, inner peace, success, amazing grace, positive energy, and an abundance of good things into my life right now.

Write this down on a piece of paper, and place it where you can see it every day. It is similar to writing the positive events that has happened in your life. Recite it with faith until it masters your thinking. Feel it as you speak, and believe the words are working for you. There is power in positive affirmations. Next have a clear vision of what you want to achieve. In my motivational speeches, I advise people to have a clear vision and purpose. If you don't know your destination, chances are you may not get there. How do you develop vision? First you must define one thing you want. Then develop passion for it. What is needed by most people in the world? How can you harness your God-given talent to alleviate this need? As you find the answers to these questions, you'll develop a mission, an action plan fueled by passion that will allow you to actualize your dreams. To have an impact on the world, you must sacrifice something; you must invest time and sometimes money, and you must muster the courage to invest with emotion and passion, with physical strength, and with a bit of mental energy.

YOUR VISION + YOUR MISSION + YOUR ACTION + YOUR PASSION = GREATNESS

What is preventing you from taking action to actualize your dreams? What are those ideas rattling inside you, wanting to shine? Today I empower you match your actions with faith. Create time every single day to do something, no matter how little, to effect change. No doubt there will be challenges on the way: people you trusted to deliver on time will frustrate your actions, become greedy with jealousy-oriented stupidity, and refuse to play their parts; your car will hit an unexpected detour, your phone will shut down, you will go broke, or a relationship will collapse unexpectedly. No matter what obstacles you encounter, understand they're all part of the creative process and are temporary. If you keep pressing on without giving up, you'll surely overcome them and reach your target. Find the positives inherent in those ups and downs, the good in the bad, and make the best use of the positives to refashion the situation to your favor. Troubling situations make you a better person by leading you to better alternatives. When things don't go well, don't trash your dreams; instead, try pushing through the challenges. The tunnel is dark and scary, but there is always a green light at the other end. You have come very far and cannot back out now. For every rejection, ask yourself what you could've done differently. If you think and pray over rejection carefully, you'll find the solutions.

To create great things, you must associate with the right people—people who will ignite the positive vibe in you. Surround yourself with supportive and progressive people who do the following:

- want to see you succeed and excel, not drain you with jealousy

- motivate you to strive to attain greater heights

- will forward your event flyers to others with excitement

- believe in you, your dreams, and your aspirations

- support you wholeheartedly

- will announce your success with excitement

- invoke spiritual energy in your life

- feel you

When I changed my thinking and started associating with people who supported and encouraged me, my life changed for the better. As I disengaged from all the negative forces in my life, moved far away from their frustrating circle, and started associating with people cheering me on, I started evolving. I rearranged myself and my passion, became more confident, and started achieving great things. A couple of years ago, I realized I needed an outside source of spiritual energy for my personal growth. I had tried to go it alone but encountered blockages that threatened my right to success. Some goals I had set up crumbled and people I had trusted failed me when I needed them most. They embarrassed me right in my face. After months of reflection, I suddenly realized that I needed to be reenergized. Then I gave my life to God. It was like a dream. I humbled myself, prostrated, and did one thing: I asked him to pilot my life's affairs, my steps, my actions, and my dreams and to reposition me for glory and place me in line for miracles. I asked for unmerited favor and gave everything that bothered me and all my challenges to him, believing he would fix them. He answered me, and this is the best thing that has ever happened to me.

My aspirations widened, my dreams brightened, and I became powerful again, with a power beyond my wildest imagination. My personality blew up, moving with the speed of light from towns to states to different parts of the world. That's when I started practically preaching to people to believe and trust God and to fix their relationships with him. When you encounter challenges in life, when you hit roadblocks, when everyone you trusted disappoints you, don't stay downcast and depressed, attracting unnecessary sympathy. Don't make that ice tea. Don't throw that pity party—you may be alone at the event. Rather give it all to God. No one is infallible. Just pick yourself up irrespective of people's reactions, dust off the dirt, restructure yourself, change your mind-set, and move on with your life, persistently asking for God's guidance. Persistence—pushing hard and firing constant shots regardless of the number of times you misfire—is the key to unlocking doors. You must hold firm even if you hit turbulence.

A few years ago, I was flying to England, and we hit waves of intermittent turbulence for about five minutes. The pilot was never perturbed; he kept a positive attitude and stayed focused and in charge, piloting calmly until we landed safely at Heathrow Airport. There in London we saluted him with applause, hugs, and handshakes. That's how life works. Never give up. It is in your power and your spiritual DNA to surmount challenges and push beyond obstacles. It is coded in your blood. You must understand that there is no standard formula for greatness. People we refer to as successful today were once like you. But they never stopped taking action or believing in themselves. They persistently evolved, even in their darkest hours. Decide today to persist to live your dream. Flush out mediocrity to increase your mobility. Don't allow any outside force or others' stupidity to distract you from living a great life or deny you the free right to creativity.

People who achieve great success are those who are constantly thinking of ways to improve their creativity. They are constantly trying new things. If you do the same, one day you'll be like them. No doubt there'll be side talk, useless comments, and disapproval. Not everyone will like you. But that's OK as long as you're moving on. Keep pushing, and don't allow negative talk to discourage you. One thing I have learned is this: whenever I am crafting a big moment and people present distractions, I usually receive abundant upliftment in my life. It may sound funny, but it's true. And it's true because the negatives make me work even harder to reach my goals and prove my critics wrong. That's the way it works.

POWER CORNER

Today I empower you to write on a piece of paper now just one goal that will change your life. Match your actions with faith, and then create time every single day to do something—no matter how little—to work on that goal to actualize that dream to change things positively around you.

THE POWER OF PRAYER: A MOVING FORCE

I GREW UP IN A SMALL village in West Africa under the strict guidance of my parents. There prayer was sacred and constant. Prayers were said every morning and each night before bedtime; we celebrated and looked forward to them. The local church situated seven miles from home was our spiritual center. At home, I never doubted the need to pray, and my mother on a daily basis stressed the importance and power of prayer, constantly reminding me that the goodness of God is unleashed through prayers. We spent lots of time doing just that—praying ceaselessly. We constantly sang joyfully while expressing a deep aura of faith. Our passion was prayer. Prayer can be personal, but it can also be done in groups and in public. Many pray at mealtimes. I say a prayer before I go out in the morning and before I go to bed at night, before I teach a class, before I take on any project, travel, drive, and before I run on the track.

I found out that if you make anything your passion, you can go far with it. That's what prayer did for me. Most things I asked for, I received. I never gave up praying; in fact, I learned to pray ceaselessly without giving up. You will never get anywhere if you stop doing what your heart is connected to doing. That is passion. For me, my heart prays every day. There is power in prayer. As a youngster I asked God for confidence, and he granted it. At the age of twelve, I read my first live lesson during the annual thanksgiving and harvest ceremony at my home church. I will cherish that memory for the rest of my life. My mother, excited and

1

humbled, gave me a big hug at the end of the holy exercise. That's the power of prayer.

Prayers work only if you believe with all your heart in whatever you pray for. Prayer has successfully uprooted loads of forgivingness and resentment and taken them away from my life, a process that still amazes me. Prayers build and solidify our trust in God and magnify our faith in the beautiful universe we are blessed with and of which we are a part. In essence, prayers mean whatever you believe for yourself, and you request that to manifest in your life. How you do it does not matter as long as it is done with faith.

The power of prayer can be seen in the lives of people who lived in ages past. Hezekiah in the scriptures provides a solid example of the power of prayer. When Hezekiah was very sick, God ministered to him through the prophet Isaiah, saying that his days on earth were limited. To many, such a message would be off-putting, heartbreaking—even traumatizing. But when Hezekiah heard this, he was neither disturbed nor worried. He never panicked. That was faith in action. Guess what Hezekiah did? He got himself together, and went into serious prayer by himself. He prayed fervently and tirelessly and gave thanks in advance for answered prayers. As a result of this spiritual marathon exercise, God heard him, blessed him, and extended his life by another fifteen years. What did Hezekiah do? He prayed, believed, and brought about change, extending his life through the power of prayer. In essence he prayed himself to life.

Prayer is the channel through which we communicate with God. Because God is invisible, we must talk to him through prayer. Prayer is practiced by different religions all over the world. Christians pray, Hindus believe in the power of prayer, and Muslims pray as well. Prayer is universal. Prayers can be said anytime, anywhere, and in many ways.

They can be said in the morning or the afternoon, at night and even at midnight. They can be said in church, in school, in the car, at the park, and even in the wilderness. The means of offering prayers can vary as well: singing, meditating, praising, and worshipping are all ways to communicate with God. Whichever way you adopt, you're praying. Prayer can also take place through thanksgiving, as a way of expressing appreciation. People say prayers for different reasons. While some pray for success, others pray for protection, strength, love, life, peace, abundance, or wealth. Some simply pray for victory. To me prayer means defining exactly what I want, holding it close to my heart, and believing wholeheartedly while giving thanks in appreciation. I give thanks both in advance for receiving exactly what I asked for and for the renewed assurance of receiving what I am expecting. Pray if you can to nourish your spiritual life and read inspirational and prayer books to sharpen your mind.

Remember Daniel, whose life was threatened by the brutal King Nebuchadnezzar following his noncompliance with the king's order. He went into a deep sleep in the presence of the hungry-looking lions. Of course Daniel knew his enemies were against him and was aware that his life was threatened, yet he was neither disturbed nor intimidated. Despite King Nebuchadnezzar's brutality, intimidating showmanship and lack of conscience, Daniel was never shaken; rather he was focused, busy planning, fortifying, and preparing himself with prayers. He chose his words boldly and carefully even when he confronted Arioch, the commander of the king's bodyguards, to ask why the king had issued harsh orders against him, his friends, and all the royal advisers in Babylon. At the end of this dangerous tribulation, David succeeded gloriously because he prayed fervently with total belief and faith in what he prayed for—victory. He never was shaken despite the risks involved; he was neither intimidated nor bamboozled by the king's military force.

When King Nebuchadnezzar realized that Daniel was being fortified by prayers to a supreme being and his predictions were coming true, the king submitted and praised God: "And now, I Nebuchadnezzar, praise, honor, and glorify the King of Heaven. Everything he does is right and just, and he can humble anyone who acts proudly" (Daniel 4:37).

With prayers, the heavens backed up the prophet Ezekiel, and he restored the dry bones. Prayer backed Peter, and he got a basket full of fishes. The apostle Paul was backed by prayers in prison, and he bounced back and singlehandedly wrote almost half of the New Testament. Remember Paul and Silas, who, while incarcerated, prayed fervently and sang nonstop. The Holy Ghost descended on them, and they received one of the most priceless gifts of humankind—freedom. Prayer changes us, our thinking, and our beliefs, and it reorganizes our focus. Prayer coupled with faith creates unimaginable outcomes. Faith is a spiritual force, the evidence of things you ask for and believe for yourself. It means believing when you pray. It blesses, honors, and creates. It sees the impossible, attracts the invincible, and creates the unimaginable. It is a force that creates avenues for receiving the unbelievable while opening doors of opportunity. Nothing is too big or too small for God to do if you pray with faith, believing and trusting wholeheartedly. If you feel God is too far away from you, then you have to rethink. You're the one who has forgotten him. He is everywhere, but you must look for him to see things move in your direction. If you remember him, he remembers you. It's that simple.

Prayer is our way of asking for blessings. It releases the spiritual force called faith, which increases the chances of receiving the things we ask for. Do not miss any opportunity to pray. If we had everything we needed, there wouldn't be any need for prayer. For me prayers shift negative situations to positive situations. When prayers are answered, miracles happen. Prayers continue to remind me that God still performs miracles. People pray for answers with different beliefs. Oftentimes they receive immediate results, but sometimes results take time. Know that if you can pray with faith and patience, you will definitely see results. God will always renew your energy, and you will draw strength from your prayer; just as we are informed in Isaiah 40:30-31-"Even those who are young grow weak, young people can feel exhausted, but those who trust in the lord for help will find their strength renewed. They will rise on wings like eagles; they will run and not get weary; they will walk and not grow weak."

The scriptures tell us that God will supply all our needs according to his riches in glory. But oftentimes we get upset that our prayers are not answered as we want. But if we were to have all our prayers answered now, what would happen to us? God in his infinite power has his own plans for us. Oftentimes we are discouraged when our dreams are not actualized or when we don't see immediate results. But understand that God may have different plans. He has a season for plowing and one for harvesting. During plowing he prepares and equips us for the harvesting time. If you are not achieving great things as you wish, don't worry. Don't be discouraged; just keep praying and pressing on. Keep a positive attitude, continue firing on all cylinders with faith, and keep working hard. In due time you will reap your rewards. No matter your dreams, no matter how impossible your goal may seem right now, pray with faith, and keep your eyes toward the miracles. In due time you'll reap blessings for your commitment. Prayer can effect change and open doors. I am a firm believer that all my success today is a product of all the genuine prayers I have offered to God, both as a child and as an adult, as well as those people have offered in my behalf. Oftentimes God blesses us for prayers offered by our grandparents or people in past generations who fervently prayed to him.

I believe God is always in the business of listening as we offer our prayers. He is always enhancing lives. Think of a child who asks his father for something. Chances are that the child will receive if he asks correctly and consistently. Likewise, God, who created us in his own image, is willing to attend to our needs. He will always answer prayers that he deems necessary and useful. Prayer improves our relationship with God just as constant communication with our parents or friends and family improves our relationships with them. With improved and progressive relationships, it becomes easier to ask for things and receive them. You gain the strength and faith to step out of your comfort zone to do things you have never done before, to take calculated risks to achieve things you never dreamed of achieving. I have learned to pray with integrity, and all my abilities. I have learned to create an intrapersonal revolution through prayer. Prayers help me create new and positive movements. They align me to achieve and attract huge blessings. They help me create a constant improvement of my life.

It has changed my life in measures I could not have dreamt of and I am full of gratitude.

Of course, to achieve great things, you must be willing to do great things. You must be strong on the inside, determined, comfortable with the unfamiliar, and ready to accept the challenges that present themselves. One simple reason most people are stuck in what they do is that they assume a repetitive pattern, over and over again, without changing frequencies. If you do the same thing all the time, by the law of repetition, you will get same results. Sometimes you need to change yourself in its entirety—your thinking, your attitude, your integrity, and your mobility. We procrastinate a lot, putting things we should've done off till eternity. Procrastination is a dream killer; it is retrogressive. To achieve things, you must eliminate procrastination. Stop postponing actions, stop rescheduling, and take positive steps to get things done. People will support you when they see you're progressing. The universe will step in to give you every single tool you need to actualize your dreams.

What is that project you have been dreaming of starting? What is that dream in your heart? What are the impediments stopping you? No matter what they are, the time to start is now. Time waits for no one. Start now to disengage and dislodge the obstacles and move on to achieve that dream. The only way not to achieve is by not starting. So start something today.

Once you begin, you'll see things shift in your favor. And when you do succeed, you must give thanks. You have an obligation to express your feelings of gratitude. Gratitude means you're appreciative. The more grateful you are, the more you pray, and the more you achieve good things. You can always express your feelings of gratitude through prayer. The expression of gratitude through prayer can positively alter the chemistry and physiology of the body; this makes you feel good and assures you that your prayers will be answered. It improves and promotes good health; it radiates healing and can cure various diseases, especially if you believe in the power of miracles. It improves the wellness of the body and soul. The life we live daily should be a life of grace and gratitude. We live on God's time. I never miss an opportunity to express my gratitude for what I have today, what I had in the past, and what I will have in the future. In fact I have cultivated the powerful habit of being extremely grateful for everything that has happened to me, both good and bad. As for the bad events, I learn from them and move on. I remain grateful for the way things happened, knowing full well that even bad situations could've been worse. For the good events, I give glory for the blessings. I bless God for everything through prayer and thanksgiving, and I have found this to be very therapeutic.

Some people pray daily. Some pray weekly, some hourly. Some do not pray at all. Some pray with passion and live their lives with passion. I pray and live every day with passion. I live with positive energy even when my prayers are not answered believing that God is still saying something. When I pray with passion and I receive, I celebrate with passion. And when I celebrate with passion, the next prayer is answered with even more blessings than I had asked for. This continues to amaze me. It works for me and will work for anyone. Develop passion no matter how rough the situation seems, and by exercising patience and believing, you'll receive. It's very easy to be stuck with impatience, but you can always overcome it. Prayer is the key with which I open all locked doors in my life. Prayer is my only channel of communicating directly with God with a view to asking for his protection while expressing my gratitude. The effects have been magnificent.

I advise you today to form the habit of being grateful for everything around you that has contributed to your personality, everything that you had in the past, and everything that comes your way. Start small, and watch the list expand exponentially. When you express your gratitude this way, you are simply saying that you appreciate what you have and will appreciate what you may receive. As you do, your capacity grows, your horizon widens, and your blessings expand. When you pray ceaselessly and act without fear or doubt, God will move in your behalf to support and help you. Don't be afraid; let nothing panic you. He will make you strong again, protect you, will bless you and save you. He has done it before and will do it again.

POWER CORNER

Start now to disengage and dislodge all the obstacles in your life and every form of negativity through the power of prayer, and move on to achieve that dream you have had all your life.

THE POWER OF DETERMINATION: A KEY TO SUCCESS

DO NOT FORGET THAT WE HAVE been commanded to be determined and confident and not be afraid or discouraged, for the Lord our God is with us wherever we go. Determination means not giving up on your dreams, no matter how tough things may seem now or how slowly you're moving. Determination is the key that unlocks the track to the finish line. Growing up in a small village in Nigeria, West Africa, I sometimes thought the world was going to crush me. However, having come from a tough background and being a product of a highly disciplined society, I knew I had the power to cruise through the hurdles of life with absolute determination. The principle of determination that I held close to my heart while growing up was imparted to me by my late disciplinarian mother, my father, and the highly structured society I found myself in during the formative years of young adulthood. These all came together to fashion the attitude of determination I have today, an attitude that has helped me, led me to various blessings, and been in general a positive force in my life.

The same determination led to the publishing of my first book and the one you are reading. The key point is this: success is a by-product of determination. Determination is a signal that if you push a little harder past the hurdle, you'll succeed. Sometimes we just want to throw in the towel when we hit a roadblock. We chicken out because we lack determination. When things get tough, you must match them with an equal toughness and push beyond the challenge. If you're willing to push just a little harder, you'll roll forward and across the finish line to victory. You'll celebrate as if you won a one-hundred-meter sprint final at the Olympics. Then you're successful.

Understand that success is relative depending on your perception. We all strive for success in our endeavors. What does success mean? Realistically success is a long journey that every individual must define based on his or her personal situation. Success for a family may mean being intact while protecting valuable core principles. Success to a student might mean being on the dean's list and passing with flying colors. For a business tycoon, success may mean having lots of money in the bank, establishing more business ventures, or being able to pay the staff a regular and fair wage. To an athlete, success may mean running at the Olympics and winning medals. Even for athletes, the road to success is never easy. It entails daily training for hours, months, and even years. For me success is not about how much money I earn as an author and speaker but how my books and positive energy help motivate people to make positive changes in their lives, including those I have touched in the smallest of ways. Whatever success means to you, it should denote accomplishment. And regardless of what you hope to accomplish, it is ideal to develop a serious affinity for whatever you do. When you love what you do, you are happy with what you create, and you'll put in your best to achieve that. Your destiny is in your hands; so too is your success. But you must be willing to work to achieve. What are you doing today? Are you limiting yourself? If so, it is time to separate yourself from that bondage. You must be determined to achieve amazing things in this place you inhabit.

Determination is the key to achieving success. It means you're pushing nonstop without giving up. It means you're willing to do your thing regardless of the challenges you encounter. I energize you to persist today to do something without quitting. When you hit a roadblock, find ways to navigate up, down, around, inside, and out of it, and then create the drive to finish. Confidence in your actions and in yourself is the greatest gift you can give yourself. Over the years I have found that many people fail because they lack self-confidence. Their resilience is weak, and they yield under tension. Their plasticity is poor, and so they chicken out easily, freeze, and give up. But I can assure you that the only way to tackle challenges to achieve success is by having confidence in yourself and working toward your plan no matter what it takes to achieve it. No matter how tough the task may be, self-confidence and determination can unlock the door to stardom. With self-confidence you affirm to yourself that you can do it without fear. Of course there will be challenges in the course of events, and at times roadblocks will seem insurmountable. I see challenges as surmountable distractions. They come in different forms. It could be a person discouraging you from pursuing your dream or trying to slow you down. It could be a friend misbehaving. It could be limited resources or a natural problem that springs up to distract you from focus. It could even be death in the family.

The key is to be patient, study how to make the right adjustments, learn something positive in the process, and then apply what you've learned to make positive changes. When faced with challenges, you must focus on the things you want to achieve. That's the key to achieving.

While at the University of Nigeria in West-Africa, during chemical titrations in the science laboratory, we looked for the end results as the acid and base mixed together in the test tubes. Our chemistry professors called this the end point. Focus on your end points, not on the reactive chemicals in the test tube. This will help you redirect your thoughts so that you have a clear idea of where to start, where to seek assistance or learn new skills, how to progress, and how to finish the project. When you ask these questions, you will start finding solutions to shift your focus from anxiety to courage. Use your creativity and imagination to help you craft powerful strategies to navigate the process. Solutions to challenges are always available within your reach, but you have to ask, search, find, and implement them wisely. Rearranging problems with a view to solving them is the key to unlocking your innate and powerful problem-solving creativity. But to create, you must possess a positive attitude.

Attitude is the key to staying focused. As humans, we have no control over the attitude of the people we come across on daily basis. You cannot control the multitude of events that make up your daily actions and reactions. Rather than trying to impress everyone around you, which can be time consuming, it's better to encourage relationships with the few who are willing to work with you to actualize your dreams. Partner with them, and harness their support to help spark the activities that will ultimately connect your ideas to your immediate surroundings and the whole world. You may even end up seeing your product or idea in the news or even better still interviewed by amazing Oprah Winfrey. How cool would that be? The key to success is to believe you can do it, recognize the challenges involved, visualize the magnitude of the obstacles, and take steps to overcome them. It entails mobilizing every human, material, and natural resource together with opportunities God puts in your path to implement the steps needed to make that big change. You must sharpen your ability to detect opportunities when they strike. Your brain constantly receives myriads of ideas. Your task is to grasp the important ones. Don't let your ideas wither inside you. Put them out for people to see, feel, and enjoy.

The universe is positioned to support and provide the basics needed for your project to take off. You can figure out the details later. No doubt you'll hit barriers, but you must look beyond them and move right

14

toward the runway to your destination. But one thing is clear: to achieve success, change is inevitable.

Oftentimes change comes with challenges. When you face challenges, you must do three things: 1. Identify the challenges, 2. Study them carefully, and 3. Find solutions to dismantle them. These critical steps will guide you in fine-tuning your energy to solve the problems. When you do, you will have abundant happiness. This is called personal achievement. I have learned that personal achievement breeds fulfillment. Physiologically, it creates positive reactions in your body chemistry and is good for your immunity and overall health. Every day we are bombarded with ideas that only need a little activation to take shape. But oftentimes these ideas are destroyed by memes that tie us down. By meme I mean a belief or an element of a culture or system of behavior that is handed down from person to person. These memes prevent us from reaching our desired goals. A meme could be as simple as a text message from one friend to another. Whatever the case, it can be retrogressive to human growth.

One simple way to dislodge memes from your mind-set is through determination—a resolution to stand your ground. Through determination you establish personal authority and stand firm. Success depends on determination to act without fear. It means believing and working tirelessly. How do you ignite determination? As I already mentioned, first decide what to work on, and write it down. One important thing I learned from my personal experience is the power of writing. Written goals are easier to work on than mental goals. When I write my goals down, I see them every day. The list serves as a constant reminder that these tasks must be accomplished. Keep your goals in a place where you can see them every day. Read them aloud every day, and meditate on them often. When you do this for some days or even months, they become part and parcel of your thought process and help you to create steps to move forward. A good idea is to first establish long-term goals. Think of how you want to be in six to ten years from now. Where do you see yourself? What title do you want added to your name? How many lives do you want to have touched? Who will you mentor? Who will you cheer on and support? When you envision these goals, you create a beautiful picture of your destination. Then set your short-term goals. These are goals that demand your immediate attention, the ones you can begin working on today that constitute the foundation for realizing the long-term goals.

The easiest and most effective way to do this is to connect with one goal and start working on it. Working on one goal rather than many at a time eliminates distractions and masks fatigue. I advise choosing the goal that resonates the most with your personality and passion, the one you approach with the most excitement. Take small actions every day to keep moving forward. Remember to evaluate your progress often. I make sure I write something every day in my manuscript and then switch to editing on the weekends. I also take weekend courses to improve my writing skills. I feel the energy of great authors; I learn from them in order to master my language, ideas, and structure. This helps to reenergize me and allows my writing skills to emerge. I motivate myself when no one else is around to do so. Do something every day to work toward your goal. As an author, when I set my goal to write this book, I ensured I was on course despite my congested schedule. No doubt there were unavoidable distractions, but I kept them to the barest minimum and focused till I published. That's the key to making things happen; the only and easiest way to make progress in whatever you set your mind on.

Understand that by doing small things consistently, you're creating a steady growth pattern.

There is so much you can do for improvement. You can read new books to improve your intellectual capabilities. You can also improve your social life; make new connections with positive people by attending social functions. You can improve your environmental capacities by looking for great opportunities that abound in society, or improve your financial stability by investing a little money in a project today. For physical improvement, you can engage in a simple exercise regimen to increase your strength and energy. Eat healthy foods, sleep well, and rest when your body needs it. Don't overwork your body. Remember, you need physical strength to achieve great things. Set your goal, dream it, constantly recite it to yourself, live it, and believe it wholeheartedly with high esteem. Avoid unrealistic or very big goals. Take them in bits, starting with the smallest ones. Though you may develop long-term goals first, you should develop smaller short-term goals to get you there. Wind up the clock of your divine energy to keep ticking; up your zeal, and fire your cylinders. Unleash emotions into your goals. Emotions can be a trigger for creative thoughts, especially when directed to your aspirations. If your emotions are negative, redirect them by thinking positive thoughts, remembering those events in your life that brought you so much joy. You can also sing a song that lightens your day or place a call to speak to a friend that brings you so much joy. Avoid anger, sadness, and depression. Stay determined. Play some good music, take a walk, run at the park, text or speak to a friend who motivates you, and you'll surely feel better. I tell people about my projects with poised belief in myself. I brand myself at all times. You can brand yourself, too. It is in your DNA and moral fibers to do so. You must talk about your goal with all your energy without minding people's reactions. You must love it for it to work. Stay focused on your goals. Celebrate every little success as you achieve results. Avoid human and nonhuman distraction. Cut off negative people from your life to avoid contamination. Some people are propellers and help you move forward. But some are chain breakers who slow you down. These individuals come with all sorts of rubbish and will never give you any useful tips to support your cause. I mandate you today to tell them, "If you don't say anything positive or act positive, get out of my territory." And mean what you say—avoid them completely. Appreciate useful people with generosity; learn from them and share your knowledge. Constantly connect with people who are positive and do the following:

- encourage you as you work on your goals to make a difference

- splash you with their positive energy

- believe in the positive move you make toward your dreams

- guide you back on track when you are drifting from set objectives

- appreciate you

- come to your aid when you are knocked out and celebrate with you when you strike it big

- feel your intentions, resonate with your principles, and believe in your movement

- are willing to tell others about your success with excitement and vigor

- support you unconditionally, without any strings or selfish motives attached.

As you do this, you create more great moments, and the universe will send more useful people and resources to assist you in achieving your goals. Don't shortchange yourself in setting great goals. Dream big, do big, act big, live big. The truth is this: people who have luck are those who dream big, work hard, and take actions with belief in themselves. They connect with opportunities because they're already prepared for them. Hard work creates beautiful opportunities. What project are you taking on today? What are you doing to make tomorrow better? What dream are you living? Dream one dream, take it head on, meditate, and let the universe feel it. Then work with determination and confidence every day, and I can assure you that you are on your way to making the big change.

As a child, I learned that money was very tough to come by and only meant for the elites. That was the belief I had. I was also taught that work is very tough. But as I got older, I found out that money was not so difficult to make. I also learned that work can be fun. I learned that money beautifies life if it is made doing something you enjoy. Then I became determined to work hard; to enjoy my jobs, my life, and everything I do; and to bless people with reckless abandon and with no reason. I decided to enjoy every day with gratitude. I had no option but to work extra hard to succeed. All human beings have the ability to improve and expand their vision. You have that energy in you. There is no limitation to your potential and no cap on how much you can achieve here on earth. You are the only one limiting yourself.

I read of a young man in his early thirties who was struck with a debilitating illness that limited his functioning to a wheelchair. He faced several obstacles in his restricted life. His greatest challenge was boredom, but he never stopped dreaming. He pushed past limitations and started writing books. Over time he self-published several books and is today living the life he desired for himself. He refused to dwell on his limitations, and this allowed him to see new possibilities and utilize his creative potential.

Rather than complaining about things that go wrong, be happy for things that went well and find something new and develop it. This will keep you renewed and help you recover faster. The human brain functions in line with the amount of stimulus it receives. When you give it positive stimuli, it generates positive thinking that brings positive actions and ultimately positive results. This means that as the human brain is put to task, its capabilities expand. This is the reason there are discoveries, inventions, new books, new dance steps, new songs, new college degrees, and new structural developments every single day. Oftentimes we are limited by our beliefs. They deny us of our free right of change and limit what we can achieve. They slow us down. But the key is this: no matter how poor your beliefs are, be determined to conquer anything you set your mind to. No matter what your desires are, you can make that quantum leap to stardom. Determine to eliminate fear from your life. What are the things you are planning to do but lack the determination? I empower you today to get them done. You will not regret it. Be realistic and focused, and take the first step. As you do, the universe will step in to support you. You will be amazed at what you can achieve with a single bout of determination.

Determination means saying or doing the right thing at the right time, irrespective of people's reactions. No matter how good you are, some people will still hate you. They'll try to pull you down to make things difficult. Even some of your allies may try to frustrate you, and people you trusted will threaten your growth. It can seem as if everyone is attempting to impede your progress. They key is this: never let them cripple your forward movement. You must not dance to their tune or allow their stupidity to derail you. You must not listen to their discouraging gymnastics. Rather, infuse high energy into your life, stay on track, gain momentum, and run past them. Remember: little minds listen, and gossip on rubbish. Big minds discuss ideas and projects. Raise your bar high, away from gossip, and set your mind on being creative and on celebrating at the finish line. That's what to do to make that positive change in the global universe of which you're a part. Some people will flow with your rhythm and dance to your tune. So connect with the people God deposits in your track, those who support you. When I started writing, I faced total discouragement from some acquaintances. If I had listened to their garbage, I may not have fulfilled my goal of becoming a published author and blessing people with the wealth of motivational knowledge that comes with my books. I would not have been blessed with the good things that I have now and may not have taken the initiative to stretch myself to further develop my power of creativity. I could have totally missed my blessings.

Determination will kill the fear of speaking boldly in public and the fear of trying something extraordinary. Determination will make you look for another job in a distant location with the mind-set that you will be successful. My choice to move from one continent to another far from home was the result of determination. When you move forward with faith and determination, the forces of the universe match your energies to see you through the turbulent zones to success. Think about the airplane. When it hits turbulence in the air, the pilot engages skills and expertise, using the various gadgets that power the airplane to alter the altitude to beat the turbulence. That's how you're structured, but you must engage your gears to fly through life's turbulence. Then God steps in to protect you and give you support, safety, and shelter. I call this the three *s*'s.

Is there something you have always wanted to do but you've been discouraged? Is there a project you have wanted to take on? I empower you today to step up in faith and start. Then watch God move those discouraging circumstances far away from you. Question every reason or excuse people give you for why you will not succeed. Once you've taken that step up and gone where you've never been before, away from your comfort zone, you've made the first move, and it won't be long before you start reaping the benefits. Determining to act without giving room for excuses is a catalyst for creativity. There is always an obstacle we think will stop us from achieving great things. But as God's people, we must act in spite of fear, uncertainties, pain, agony, inconvenience, or the number of days, months, or years it'll take to reach our goals. Just express your belief in yourself and in your drive to succeed.

Self-expression is an energy booster that provides you with extra strength to work harder while creating the drive and the means to succeed. It rejuvenates your system to remove fearful thoughts. If you start bringing together piece by piece every tool you need, over time you'll discover that you won't use every single tool. But those utilized should be implemented maximally as the solid foundation for strength, balance, and the energy needed to project your strategy to fruition.

One powerful strategic key to determination is to present your goal to the public even before you start. When you do that, you hold yourself responsible to deliver and leave no option other than to pull through. When I nursed the ambition of becoming a published author, I was prepared in my mind but lacked the drive to make the first move. A few weeks later, with no master plan, I went ahead using word of mouth to inform friends, neighbors, coworkers, and even random people I met on the street about my project. I gave out business cards in advance with information on the projected release date. Some low-minded people dismissed the idea on the spot. But I never listened to their garbage because I was determined to create something that would bless humanity. I knew what I wanted to achieve and did my thing, knowing full well my books would inspire and motivate someone, somewhere, someday— and they're doing just that. With the toughness I learned from my late mother, I knew nothing would ever stop me, not even utterances from vision killers. I wrote on a piece of paper things to do and gathered every tool needed to actualize the dream. Then I dusted my computer, gave thanks in advance, embraced the inspiration to write and started typing. I was determined to create something. Though some people dismissed the idea on the spot and gave it no chance of succeeding, others encouraged me to start immediately with a thumbs-up. Having broadcasted my plan to the outside world, I had no option but to start working right away. A few years later, my life expanded drastically beyond my wildest expectations, and the rest is history.

What is the lesson here? I was determined. I took off flying. And new things started happening. I did not let the idea fizzle out. It is always exciting to embrace new things, but it takes determination and sacrifice to be successful. It takes a strong and brutal mentality to create success. Declare a total war against every obstacle you encounter until you achieve victory. It is not always easy to break through, but with determination you'll succeed. Oftentimes the road brings stop signs, potholes, and detours, but if you are willing to continue pushing with determination, you'll navigate out of them and will sure see the light shining before long. It takes discomfort to create comfort. If you want to expand your horizon, you must welcome discomfort; you must be willing to come out of your comfort zone. This may involve connecting with people whom ordinarily you would not have met. Be confident and respectful when you associate with them. Be sure they're positive-minded people who connect with your spirit, not people who will poison your energy by reminding you of the negative consequences of starting a project. To experience growth and success, you must change something. You must brace yourself for the challenges, too. Usually you feel uncomfortable when you try something for the first time but as you progress you'll start to get comfortable with the act and progress faster.

Let me say this. Inside the difficult lies the miraculous. Discomfort is stressful, but it is a positive sign that changes in your favor along the way, if only you believe and work hard with determination. Every act is tough at the beginning. But as you practice, it becomes easier, and over time you become a champion. Repetition creates perfection. My first motivational speech was a big challenge. But as I spoke more, I gained confidence and eventually became comfortable enough to minister to hundreds of people. Growth follows tough situations. Instead of retreating when you are uncomfortable, make a solid declaration to proceed, knowing that you're creating positive changes.

Determination does not work unless you have goals. Having a goal means having an end in mind. But developing your goals can present challenges. One of the biggest mistakes that people make is setting goals that are very overwhelming. It is advisable to start with the small things and work gradually and systematically toward the big plan. That way you are not overwhelmed by the demands, and you are more able to tackle the challenges piecemeal. If your goal is to work as a teacher, you must go to school, buy the books, take the classes, and pass all your tests to qualify before teaching. The same principle applies in life. You must do small things consistently with a view to reaching your target goal. This way the challenges that come up are small and within your solving capacity, making it easier to stay motivated as you progress. Never fail to motivate yourself, even when no one is cheering you on.

Oftentimes people find themselves in situations where no one motivates them. A lack of external motivation is meaningless unless you give it meaning. You can motivate yourself. Talk to yourself as if someone else is talking, and in no time you will need no one to cheer you on. Your self-motivation will become a motivational force in your daily life, inducing extra energy into your system. I do it all the time, and it works. Self-motivation is powerful and gets you going. Ask yourself some questions: Where do I want to be in three years? How do I improve my discipline? How do I enhance my self-worth? Answering these questions will not only empower you but will stretch your mind. Daily efforts enhance confidence, build determination, and create instrumental success stories that help build self-esteem and inspire you to bigger responsibilities. This creates a monumental effect. Ask yourself serious questions about how you can do some beautiful things; increase your self-worth, values, and principles to better your life with a view to living your dream. To increase your chances of succeeding, you must be willing to expand your focus and redirect your thoughts toward only what is important.

POWER CORNER

When change makes you uncomfortable, instead of retracing your steps, make a powerful declaration to fire on, to push harder, and to continue moving on, believing that you are expanding your capacities for personal growth. Before long you'll see that proverbial light at the end of the tunnel.

THE POWER OF CONNECTIONS: NETWORKING TO EXPAND

MAKING CONNECTIONS MEANS LINKING WITH YOUR thoughts and your passion. It means joining with the right people to take advantage of opportunities. Life is about connecting with people. But it is also about making a connection with ourselves— also means listening to that inner voice constantly talking to us especially in the early hours of the morning when you can hear a pin drop.

One important aspect of connections is the ability to master your instincts—the voices instructing you to act, that speak to you prior to making decisions. Instinct is the voice mandating you to make a move when others are standing still, the voice telling you to talk or keep quiet, to take a new class, sing a song, entertain in public, initiate a movement, change your location, start a business, or create that positive change that will bless billions of people worldwide. Listen to that voice. That's the voice of wisdom, progress, confidence, creativity, and connection. That's the voice of God.

Oftentimes we want God to physically appear to us before we connect with that voice. But God connects to us by speaking, the same way he spoke to the prophets of old. Therefore, you must be willing to listen when he speaks. That is the voice connecting you to a new level. It speaks to us, providing instructions, but at times we don't listen or believe the power in his words. When God gave

Moses a power, Moses did not believe he was already blessed to lead his people and leave an everlasting legacy. He was too busy asking irrelevant questions and seeking people's approval. "Suppose the people do not believe me and will not listen to what I say?" he asked. Despite the walking stick in his hand, he still doubted his power until God asked him to drop it to the ground, where it was transformed into a snake. To further demonstrate his unbelief, Moses took off. Sounds funny, right? On God's instruction he picked up the snake by its tail, and it became a stick again. That was when he believed. Moses was mesmerized by many other events that proved to him that God was speaking. Do you want to wait longer before connecting when God speaks? I would bet the answer is no. God is in the business of constantly appearing and speaking, but you must be ready to connect. God is constantly connecting us with people he carefully selects to bring relief to us. He has a unique way of doing his thing. He places people strategically in our lives for a purpose. When David felt lonely, God provided Jonathan. When Abraham and his beautiful wife, Sarah, were becoming frustrated with Sarah's barrenness, he produced Isaac. Do not forget that this ancient couple were in their old age when God moved to increase their family numbers. When Ruth felt battered, barren, bereaved, and broken, God connected her to Naomi, who mentored her to glory. When Naomi and Ruth were finding life unbearable, he introduced Boaz, who owned a large expanse of land and was comfortable and rich. Then things changed for the better, and they started living large, enjoying life again. God has already planned the connections he will put in your life to bring that change. Just be patient. Be in an attitude of expectancy, be alert to know when they show up, and be ready to connect with the beautiful angels he deposits in your path.

Connecting with your passion, the powerful force inside you, is a means to creativity. It is the process through which we connect with our designated calling. Some are called to preach, some to sing, some to write, some to dance, some to cook, some to run. Your passion is your calling, the thing you love to do no matter the constraints. If you're passionate about cooking, that's your calling. If you're passionate about dancing, that's your calling. Go for it. Let your passion guide you to your creative power. Is there something you enjoy doing for fun? Is there something inside you that you love and are good at that is begging to come out to shine for the world? That's your passion, the creative energy within you waiting to be ignited. Let it shine regardless of people's reactions. Be focused about it, and do your thing. You will definitely reap the benefits if you don't give but continue working diligently to make that change.

If you want to be successful, find something you enjoy doing, and then follow your heart's direction. If you want to be a dancer, dance like you have four PhDs in dancing. If you are a singer, sing as if your mother is the one dictating the tune. If you're a motivational speaker like me, speak everywhere, including in the kitchen, whether someone is cooking or not. There is something amazing about passion. I have tried to understand the principle but cannot. But I know one thing—it's powerful, and I am benefiting from it. Your passion is your love for what you do, and it can change things in your life to translate into success. The more passion you inject into your movement, the more the forces of the universe lead you to creating unbelievable things. Success involves doing something new and at times launching a surprise project. No matter the definition, it involves action. You must take action and push beyond the obstacles to produce a reaction. Once you do that, people will react and connect. Some will try to poison your vision. Others will offer support to move you to the next level. Connect with the later, and shine as you approach your next project. Every great feat is the result of an idea that ran contrary to the norm. Develop your ideas, keep up the vibe as you progress and your connections will provide the necessary creativity to unleash that positive force into the universe to achieve greater things.

Creativity involves stepping away from the usual to challenge yourself to something new or connecting with something that seriously needs your time, commitment, investment, and divine energy. Shine the light deposited inside you to make a change in your world. There must be a shift to create a gift. Something must give. I love soccer, and I love watching a great match. When a game gets tough, the team with the skills and energy takes the game to the next level and outshines the opponent to score the goal to victory. The same applies to life. You must be ready to step up your game to unleash that winning shot. Sometimes we get too cool and comfortable with our mediocre status, our local champion position, our old lifestyle, or our location. Don't. You have to be constantly evolving. I succeed more when I introduce some positive radicalism contrary to the conventional pattern. When I do something unexpected but powerful to skyrocket myself out of my comfort territory, I see amazing results. To get this book out to billions of people around the world, I woke up in the middle of the night to write. I paid a price, losing more than two hours of sleep each night during the time the project lasted. That was the game plan because I needed to wrap up and create the next movement. To make a change, you must have courage, energy, and the vibe. You must deal with the challenges that accompany the process. Do not fear the hurricane or the tornado; rather, learn how to recover after the devastating storm. You must display spirited radicalism to achieve the impossible and see things move toward you. You must be willing to do extraordinary things.

I like giving. It is one of my passions. Ask me for help, and it's done. Ask me to help jump-start your car, and I do a quick dance and help. I may not always be able to give what is asked, but I must do something if not immediately but later. How did I develop this passion? I connect to an inner voice that instructs me to give at the least opportunity. This has become part and parcel of my personality. It inspires me and has taken me places. In fact, it created the drive to write this self-help book to assist and guide people toward making serious positive changes in their lives. That is connection. What is that passion begging for connection within you? The human mind is bombarded with voices constantly speaking to us. Have you thought of giving them some force? Be assured that one will connect with you to make that needed change.

In psychology, we learn that we are a product of our mental connections and that ideas are first initiated in the mind, a functional part of the brain. Many people go through life trying to connect with their mind. They keep trying, planning, and studying, but eventually they give up. Connecting with your mind is the first step to energizing yourself for a purpose-driven life. How do you connect with your mind? First, pay attention to how you feel on the inside. There is always a spot inside everyone that speaks to you from time to time. It is a spontaneous voice that speaks to you at any time but you must be alert to listen when it speaks. Is there a time you feel like there is a voice speaking on the inside directing you on what step to take or what route to avoid. If you listen carefully, you will hear and if you follow the directions, you will make decisions that exactly match the instructions from your inner voice. Secondly, follow your instincts, an inheritable tendency to make very specific response to environmental stimuli without involving serious reasoning. Simply stated, it is a behavior that you exhibit below the conscious level and can be automatic but very powerful and rewarding. Your instincts guide you but you must be willing to listen. We are a product of our thoughts and instincts. Thirdly and finally work on what your instincts tells you and hold on to the knowledge to expand it on regular basis. Over time it becomes part and parcel of your life and your growth process expands rapidly because you will make better decisions and take proper actions to achieve great things. Whatever we give access to, our mind manifests in the way we plan, think, or execute projects. Your mind is the stepping-stone for success. Most people are infested with negative thoughts throughout their lives, some with positive thoughts. Either way, you get what you feed your mind. But it is better to feed your mind with positive stuff for positive outcomes.

Create commitments with people you meet. If you can get people to commit, they'll likely build great relationships and do things for you. Offer solutions where possible. People will feel comfortable with you if they are sure you're willing to offer some help. If you're positive, people will connect and stick with you. No one wants to associate with someone who is always negative. Associating with people with good reputations also improves your own reputation. If your life is negative, please examine yourself and remove all forms of negativity from your system, your actions, your intentions, activities and mobility.

Connecting with people means cooperating with them. How do you connect? People will like you if they're comfortable being around you. If you can make them smile or laugh or just feel good, they will open up their hearts and support you when you need their help. First impressions are important. When you make a good first impression, you connect better. You open people's hearts to listen to you, especially if you respect them. When you respect people, they reciprocate. No matter how successful you are, you must respect others. If you respect people, they'll feel respected, and you'll build a powerful connection. Appreciation builds rapport. Every effort people make to assist you must be appreciated with humility and gratitude. Encourage people in your circle and avoid envy.

Envy ruins relationships, so avoid jealousy completely. The best way to free yourself is to recognize it. Understand that you are not singled out for problems. Recognize that you are the one who controls your attitude. Remind yourself that jealousy is a poison that saps your energy. Set the track you want your life to take irrespective of outside influence. Live the way you want (positive ways, anyway), not the way others want. Avoid interference. If you don't create a clear plan and a system of action, then be ready to be enslaved by the selfish intentions of people's stupidity. Stay connected to your core values while making progress and utilizing available resources. See opportunities everywhere. Identifying and utilizing opportunities will constitute the guiding light of illumination that will pilot you to a life of abundance. There are golden opportunities everywhere, but you have to see them to make the move to grab them. Regain control of your life, change your attitude, and avoid negative thoughts. Start speaking positive words, take positive actions, and radiate positivity at all times—even at rest. If stress contributes to your negativity, take a break from the source of the stress. In the early morning, meditate on the good things that have happened in your life. This will help to counter some of the negativity and alleviate stress to put you in a positive mind set throughout the day. It is OK to flush out all negative people from your life and connect with people who are happy, excited, focused, and supportive—people who want to see you succeed. Plant an attitude of success in your mind by talking only positives.

To make people connect with you, you have to feel with their worries. When asked, assisting a person to get back to terms by using encouraging words will help seal a better bond. Just as negativity is toxic, so too is associating with negative people. Connecting with people is awesome, but avoid connecting with negative people. Their negativity can be harmful. You are at liberty to make a choice. I simply keep away from negative people or when unavoidable I relate to them from a distance. I send a clear message signaling we cannot work together. Irrespective of your age, you are always free to choose your friends. None of them is attached to you forever. You can always make new friends who are willing to support you. Understand that you have the ability to change any situation if you are willing to. Sometimes negative people are our family members. A good thing to do to avoid their contamination is to move away from them and associate less often with them. You can always choose who you deal, associate, and communicate with. The choice is yours. When you create a positive lifestyle, every person and every energy around you revolves around positives, and you can then channel your life the right way. If you have positive energy, you have no tolerance for negative people, you radiate positivity, and the universe attracts more positive things and people to you. One thing to keep in mind is honesty. Honesty has power. People around you will connect better if you're honest. It builds their trust. People respect and value honesty.

When I decided to perform a turnaround maintenance in my life, I created a mental refurbishing of my personality by changing my modus operandi. I made a commitment to reorganize and rewrite the history of my life. I developed a zero-tolerance policy for negative people, raising the bar so that they cannot get near me to avoid their contamination. My life took a positive turn. Things started working in my favor. If you want to see great things happen in your life, hang around positive people. Positivity breeds success. Partnering with positive people enhances success because their positivity rubs off on you when you're in their presence.

The circumstances that keep you unhappy can always be altered. How you internalize, process, and craft the means to change the situation depends on your attitude. A positive attitude requires you to be proactive in making decisions and taking actions. It is better to be proactive than reactive when you face challenges. Being proactive enhances success. Success depends on what you do or what you don't do. You can do anything you set your mind to. You have the energy, skills, ability and the resources to work with. God created the universe with everything we need to operate and succeed, but whether you succeed depends on your use of the tools he provides. It depends on how you utilize the universal abundance and whether you change gears when necessary. If you continue applying the same tactics, you'll get the same results. Do something new to make something great. When you succeed in one act, you must advance to the next level. Success is for people who plan systematically and are productive and hardworking. It is for those who change frequencies easily and are willing to take risks. You are destined to do big things, so plan better today to reach your greater tomorrow. Planning is paramount in making progress. Remember the popular saying: if you fail to plan today, you plan to fail tomorrow. So it will sure do you some good to plan for the future today.

I tap inspiration from the story of Joseph, who made Pharaoh understand that blessings come from God. He explained his dreams to him concerning the seven years of famine followed by seven years of abundance in Egypt. He told Pharaoh what God had planned and advised him to build massive barns, make warehouses of food, and store grains and instructed him on how to prepare and save for the rainy days. Despite his high handedness and intimidating personality, Pharaoh listened and planned ahead, respecting Joseph's instructions. When the famine hit as predicted, there was serious food scarcity all over the world—except in Egypt. When Joseph's father heard there was grain in Egypt, he said to his sons, "Why don't you do something? I heard there is grain in Egypt, go there and buy some to keep us from starving to death"(Genesis 42:1–2).

They went to Egypt and met their brother Joseph, who was the governor in charge. What did they do? They took action and were blessed with food and the golden opportunity to reconnect with their brother they had ostracized, humiliated, and left to die. They traveled to Egypt despite the risks, defied every obstacle, shifted grounds, and were not stopped by resistance. The key word to learn here is preparation. Is there something you've wanted accomplished but have put off preparing for it? Is there a song you want to sing, an instrument you want to play, a trip you want to embark on, or inspiration you want to impart into others? The time to prepare is now! Don't let your energy, songs, ideas, and stories die inside you. Poet Maya Angelou said, "There is no greater agony than bearing an untold story inside you." Tell that story today. It'll take you to places you've never imagined. That's how life works. I don't care what you are going through today. If you stay faithful, there is nothing too hard for God to start in your life. He is in the business of restructuring people and you'll not be an exception.

As an author, I travel frequently, speak in public, and meet many people. In the process, I ask lots of questions and have realized that resistance is the number one thing that stops people from living their dreams. Resistance, in any of its different forms, will tell you nonsense to keep you from doing something. It will make you comfortable in your situation. Resistance will reason things out with you like a professor to keep you from personal advancement. Have you ever felt overwhelmed when you wanted to take on a big project? Have you ever felt like quitting even before you started? Have you ever felt like you failed the test even before the examination? If your answer is yes, you have yielded to resistance. How do you eliminate resistance?

Understand that God has created and endowed you with a very strong vibe of divine energy to do great things that only you can initiate and do while you still live. In my life so far, I have learned interesting lessons that have helped reshape me on my journey. One is that self-motivation is the most honest encouragement that you can ever have. You must constantly motivate yourself and stop seeking approval from others. If you love your acts and they're beneficial to you and humanity, keep doing what you're doing. Stop taking unnecessary precautions because you're influenced by the thoughts of destiny killers. Live the life that will change your standards for good. Remember, life is yours and must be lived to the fullest. You may experience hard times and turbulent waves before achieving. But no matter how tough life is, I advise you to never give up. Be totally committed. The universe provides the human and capital resources you need to press on. So take off like a supersonic jet to live your dreams.

POWER CORNER

Negativity slows down success. It is poisonous. Flush out negativity from your mind-set, mobility, and mentality today, and you'll see amazing things happening in your life.

THE POWER OF MEDITATION: SOOTHING THE SOUL

MEDITATION IS THE ACT OF BEING still and provides a channel through which to connect with your peaceful location. Meditation aligns us to connect with our thoughts under the influence of the stillness of our mind. Meditation is mentally and spiritually therapeutic and sharpens our wellness. The best way to meditate is to identify one thing and focus deeply, feeling it until it manifests. It may be a desire, a dream, a vision, a plan, or even a person whom you want blessings extended to. Meditation brings a revolution of the mind, produces a clear revelation of hidden things, and engages your heart to search for answers that add value to life.

Meditation rejuvenates our souls, directs our thoughts to God, moderates our impulses, fine-tunes our moral conscience, and creates focus in our subconscious minds. Meditation clarifies and provides solutions by translating quiet thoughts into reality. It lowers blood pressure and pulse rate, relaxes nerves, relieves stress, and calms the whole body. Meditation harnesses positive energies in the body into one, creating a mind-body connection.

To practice meditation, first designate a comfortable area without distractions. You can listen to background music. Some exercise before meditating is OK for relaxing your body. Wear lose clothing to create a mental impression that you're free and ready to flow with the rhythm.

Then take a deep breath to relax your body. Next, define one thing you really want in your life and direct all your attention and energy to it while keeping silent but with absolute focus on that which you want. Think about that with your whole heart and make positive declarations invoking that right into your life. You can say a little prayer to back your thoughts up afterwards. Start by focusing on one thing and over time switch to different things at same time. Meditation doesn't have to last for hours; just a couple of minutes can create focus. Practicing for ten, fifteen, or twenty minutes is a good way to start. When you meditate you shut off worries, release divine energy, and connect to the Supreme Being.

Meditation doesn't have to be personal. You can meditate on your life, your health, your family, or your friends. You can meditate on inspiration, academic pursuits, your profession, or the society of which you're an integral part.

Meditation quickens dream manifestation by allowing you to talk to yourself about reasons your dream will be actualized, feel the inherent possibilities, and gain the motivation to begin or continue working toward its accomplishment. You can use visualization and meditation to make your dreams a reality. Your thoughts have energy and attract what you focus on. So be careful what you think. Our thoughts are either negative or positive, and the mind reproduces what it is fed, reflecting back negative or positive effects on us.

Start meditating by planting good thoughts in your mind. Then vocalize those thoughts to release creativity. Declare them in your life, expect the best things, and you'll see them manifest. I meditate on my life, my job, my business, my family, my friends, and my sense of smell, vision, voice, and hearing. I meditate on the nation, for peace in the world, and for the poor. I meditate on our pastors, our president, the homeless, seniors, the rich, the children, the poor, and on our soldiers who protect us and our sovereignty. I meditate more on others than on myself, and my spiritual growth is sharper. The effects have been enormous. It is like praying for the whole world of which you are a part of. Whatever blessings you pronounce to the world come back to you because you are part of that world. When you meditate, you allow your inner self to speak to you.

Decide today to create time for meditation. Meditation redirects your path to your passion. Everyone models greatness, but there is no great person who doesn't aspire and work hard to be one. There is no standard formula for choosing a profession. You choose what you like or what people see in you. Sometimes others can see what you don't. However you connect with your profession, believe it, and meditate it into fruition. Everyone has dream and aspirations. Your success is directly proportional to the work you put in. Hard work precedes success and produces a sensational feel-good high. Is there a better feeling than seeing your personal accomplishments? I doubt it.

Meditation ignites the latent fire inside us. The best time to listen to your soul is when you are meditating. During this time I advise you to listen to your heart and find out what makes your heart fuzzy—what ignites your spiritual fire. Our heart encourages us during this process, cheering, inspiring us, and begging for our connection to do the things our mind directs. Don't be vague in your focus. Be very specific so you can feel the solutions. Specificity means seeing yourself in the exact state, feeling and living it.

Visualize important things; pay less attention to insignificant details. For example, if you desire to be in love again, visualize being in a wonderful relationship full of love. Avoid dwelling on a failed relationship, forcing love on someone who doesn't like you, or crying endlessly over an expired relationship. I am sure you get it. The excitement you want from a new relationship lies within you, and there is no reason to look elsewhere for it. You can attract and create one. Give love, and love will chase you. Show love, and love will show up for you. Always search your heart to ask yourself the purpose of your life. Ask what makes you happy and what you can do to maximize your energy to beautify your life. Meditation will answer these questions and will redirect you from a hopeless situation to an enviable one and connect you to any position in the spiritual realm that you want to assume.

Once you connect with your purpose, the next step is to follow through with what you want to do, be it starting a business, writing a song, completing high school, going to college, planting a tree, starting a charitable foundation, enrolling in a dance class, championing a movement for the homeless, or playing the recorder or piano in your home church band. You can excel at anything you set your mind to if you inject poise and passion.

The secret to success is the passion you exude, the work you put in, and your showmanship, which is a function of your poise. Connecting with your thoughts is the first step in changing your life by changing your awareness, giving you the opportunity to put information together. During this time your thoughts work in consonance with your peaceful mind. Then you can develop solutions to challenges and give birth to ideas that enhance your life to set new goals.

Today I enjoin you to start meditating. Meditate that your heart, lungs, brain, veins, and every organ in your body are working at maximum efficiency. Speak health into your life as you meditate for the vigor and vitality of your body, the engine room of your mobility. Meditate on your goals often. Setting goals and writing them down is not enough. You have to meditate on them. Injecting life into your goals is important as well. You must do something consistently to bring them to fruition. Oftentimes work is tough, and that's when some people chicken out, resign to fate, and give up. Don't stop; continue believing in your dreams while trying new things with different mind-sets. Then incorporate fearlessness.

Relax often and ward off anxiety. Anxiety is a false presentation designed to frustrate you. Disconnect anxiety from your mind. You're an overcomer manufactured in the image of the most high, so why worry and destroy your spiritual foundation with fear? Believe in yourself. There is power in belief. Barack Obama believed he would be the first African American president of the United States. He was determined, worked hard, and defied every distraction. He refused to be intimidated by racial differences and manipulations. He believed he could succeed by doing things that needed to be done, things that mattered most. You don't have to aspire to be the president, a world boxing champion, or a Nobel Prize laureate (though there's nothing wrong with that), but you can determine to succeed in anything you focus on.

I empower you to be fully committed both emotionally and physically to live your dream. Get up every day and do something, whether you feel good or not. When you do, you set the pace to create opportunities that open the doors of success. You change your today for a greater tomorrow. Creating dreams requires follow-up. Dreaming without following through is like not dreaming at all. You must build a framework upon which your thoughts can stand and have confidence in your belief. Your imagination when matched with good intentions and propelling actions produces great achievements. Your feelings have latent energy and internal vibrations. Like a magnet, they possess powerful energy. Initially the energy is hidden, but with the right injection of actions, it metamorphoses into kinetic energy, the energy that inspires you to do things, the energy that produces results. Kinetic energy is always in motion, and it creates success. So if you're blessed with good energy, please celebrate it. I celebrate mine every single day. It energizes me to achieve and I am very grateful for the energy God has given me.

Action creates reactions. Not all your actions will succeed, but even if you fail, understand that it is OK to fail. It is part of life. It means you're bold and doing things. You cannot fail without trying, so failure is a positive thing. You either fail or win. There cannot be failure without a preceding action. But to succeed, you must be disciplined. In this life, I have learned that it takes discipline to achieve success. The world's most respected and greatest success stories stay disciplined and focused and never stop concentrating on set targets, a powerful trick to maintaining success. It is very easy to be distracted by people, events, or negative actions, but when you push beyond the distractions with discipline, you'll succeed in measures that attract the attention of good people. Oftentimes you may even launch a global movement. Guess what? You're now a success story. If you're willing to give your actions your time and energy and believe in yourself, you will be amazed by how you transform. Your positive actions can change your life forever. Sometimes it is just about doing something very little but consistently. Small things done consistently with passion and energy metamorphose into big things.

I draw inspiration from the Prophet Elisha's belief in the power of small things. After Naaman was infected with leprosy, Elisha simply instructed him to wash himself in the River Jordan to be cured. Recall that Naaman was a powerful person in the Syrian military, an influential force, and he did not want to come into contact with the very dirty River Jordan. As a leader, Naaman thought it was dehumanizing, absurd, insulting, and degrading. It took his assistant months to convince him to act as Elisha had instructed. When Naaman finally did wash in the River Jordan, he was totally healed of leprosy. Can you imagine simply washing in a river bringing healing? That is the power of small belief. The same principle still applies today. You can receive blessings, healing, joy, peace, happiness, promotions, and so many other good things if you're willing to do small things with faith. Never underestimate the power of small acts. I know there is power in small things, and I believe in it. Some little things you have not thought of doing may be keeping you from good things. Change that today. Do some little things with obedience. You will see things shift positively in your direction. The universe has been around since the beginning of God's creation. So many resources exist—the air, cars, houses, trees, soil, love, people, energy, happiness, peace, and life, to mention but a few. Your duty is to harness this abundance of resources with their connecting possibilities to create the life you want. Think creatively to create big.

There is power in creative thinking. Being a practical living example, I will give a brief synopsis of my life to buttress my point to empower you. I grew up in Eastern Nigeria, a giant country in the western part of the African continent. As a youth, I dreamed of living and working in the United States. I needed more opportunities for personal growth and advancement. I needed a change of scene to make a positive change in the global universe. So I sent out a message about my intentions: I told God about them. I felt my desire, prayed tirelessly, meditated, dreamed it, and believed it. I started feeling joy in my heart and gave thanks in advance for answered prayers. I was full of gratitude. Then, from out of the blue, an idea came. I played the diversity lottery program and followed through with prayers and utmost belief, and my wish came to pass: I won, processed my visa and I am living in the United States. The opportunity I asked for in America was one that led to the creation of this book and other things for which I am very grateful. The universe has blessed me immensely, and I am joyful for its wonders. God has been so good to me, and I thank him every day. I have always wanted to be an author. Initially it seemed like an unrealizable dream. But as I started to visualize it, I developed absolute confidence that I could and would make it happen. Then an inspiration came again. I gathered all the necessary materials, bought a hard drive and an advanced computer, and started typing away. I totally changed the way I thought about authors. I mentally arranged all the publishing companies I knew and spoke to them mentally. I took action, and the rest is history. What did I do? I believed and made it happen. The universe reflects exactly what you think and hold closely to your heart. It is there for us to work with. It is working in consonance with our beliefs and thought processes. It will work for you if you believe and trust God.

POWER CORNER

Meditation is the time to visualize your life, connect with your soul, and assume any position with authority in the spiritual realm that you want for your life. Start meditating today; you'll be amazed with the benefits.

THE POWER OF EXERCISE AND GOOD FOOD: FOR OPTIMAL HEALTH

EXERCISE IS ONE OF THE BEST natural medicines. The benefits are unquantifiable. Most forms of exercise are surprisingly inexpensive. For example walking, a free form of exercise requires no equipment or special training. It can be done at the park, at work on your lunch break, or even in your backyard. Exercise strengthens the muscles throughout the whole body and improves lung and heart functions. Exercise enhances productivity and improves confidence. With a healthy body, you can achieve so much.

You don't have to wait until you weigh 260 pounds with sagging skin folds and layers of fat to start exercising. You know that such a state is detrimental to health. Exercise should be a regular, structured program in your life. If you're overweight, don't lose hope or give up; get focused on eating right and exercising to lose weight. Losing weight isn't as tough as people think. With the right approach, you can achieve weight loss. One very important area in the human body is the waistline, the area closest to your belly. Belly fat is close to the vital organs and is the most dangerous fat in your body. Excess belly fat is a warning sign of more serious health challenges to come, including diabetes, heart disease, and even some forms of cancer, all of which are very avoidable with a good exercise regimen, healthy dietary habits, and serious lifestyle changes.

Incorporating exercise into your life can have very positive effects, even seemingly small exercises like walking up the stairs instead of taking the elevator whenever you can. A fifteen-minute walk every day adds up to overall health. Do not discard the importance of exercise. I know a young obese man who had proven very difficult to convince of the importance of exercise. Efforts made to encourage him to walk for at least ten minutes three times a week fell on deaf ears. It was not until he had his first heart attack at the age of forty-seven that he reversed his lifestyle to incorporate some exercise, and since then he has had more strength, more motivation, and more drive and alertness. As a result, he's become more productive at work and has increased energy levels. A heart attack was the crisis he needed to make that positive move, but you don't want to wait to have health issues to decide to engage in a healthy exercise regimen. Personal developments often emerge as a result of hardship, but it's better to be proactive and not reactive, which in this case means taking preventive measures. Being proactive is part of the growth process and requires using every difficult experience to learn. You must learn from past experiences. If you don't learn, you'll never grow, and you'll paralyze your ability to improve. That's not fair to you.

As I mentioned earlier, walking is very good for you. It is essentially a free massage for the body, and it strengthens the legs, muscles, and bones, promoting bone calcification. The latter is especially important for women, who are at a higher risk for osteoporosis. Walking also builds cardiovascular endurance. Every minute of walking offers powerful benefits to your body. Studies have shown that people who walk regularly not only weigh less but have higher self-esteem and better overall lifestyles. It's advisable to start small and exercise with patience, awaiting the desired benefits. I encourage you to keep walking because good health is the best insurance you can ever have. Exercise helps relieve depressive moods. When you exercise, the body releases chemicals called endorphins. These are natural pain killers and they work with the receptors in the brain that reduce how you perceive pain thus starting a wave of positive feeling in your body. This is the same type of feeling you have after running, and it has positive effects on the body. It also energizes your body and gives you a sense of improved self-esteem creating a positive outlook to things. These endorphins also act as natural sedatives (substances that make you relax and sleep) which explain why you sleep well after a bout of intense exercise. Create time for a daily routine of exercise. Take a walk outside to energize while breathing fresh oxygen. Running at the track and lifting small weights are good activities for strength building, and they also keep you recharged, excited, and motivated. Feeling tired and drained all the time is a sign of burnout; it means you are not taking good care of yourself.

Another tool for good health is eating healthy foods. We are taught in school to eat food composed of the three basic components—carbohydrates, fats and oils, and protein. Good food is a vital factor for a healthy life. A body deprived of good food does not thrive and may not think well. It is advisable to eat foods that have the three basic components, including lots of vegetables and fruits, and to drink the right amount of water daily. Half your body weight in ounces of water every day is advisable, although some advice six to eight glasses daily. Good carbohydrates to consume are those that are not bleached—for example, whole-wheat and whole-grain products. Bleached carbohydrates products can lead to weight gain, causing obesity and other complications that could impair bodily function. Start eating healthy today, stop procrastinating by making excuses, for procrastination leads to failure.

Fruits are an important aspect of good nutrition. Many fruits contain high amounts of vitamin C, a substance that fights free radicals in the body and helps in wound healing. Free radicals are disease-causing organisms in the body that are linked to cause some cancers. Fruits are also packed with antioxidants and other vitamins that are very good for the body. Some vitamins can boost the levels of HDL, the "good" cholesterol. The apple is a fruit that offers these benefits. It lowers the level of the bad cholesterol and increases the good. Oranges, grapes, and many vegetables have lots of vitamin C. While a daily intake of fruits and vegetables helps improve health, eating the right amount can be difficult. One way to do so is to blend the different fruits together into a smoothie. With the adequate amount of vitamins in your body, you'll feel stronger and more able to tackle your day's activities. Eating fish and nuts is also a good idea. These foods provide the body with powerful omega-3 fatty acids that support heart functions. A daily serving of a variety of nuts can help lower blood pressure as well. Nuts also help maintain glowing skin, improve memory, and can help with depression. Salmon, another food rich in omega-3 fatty acids, helps with moods, too.

Iron—a powerful component of hemoglobin, the protein that transports oxygen through the whole body to produce energy—is a powerful component of good nutrition. Certain foods contain high amounts of iron, for example egg yolk, beans, chick peas, dried fruits including prunes and raisins, broccoli, kale, spinach, liver and some cereals and raisins. These foods are rich in iron and are highly recommended. The body depends on oxygen to function maximally. When depleted of iron, the body feels tired and may not be strong enough to carry out daily activities. A person with low iron may think faultily and make poor choices. An iron deficiency can also lead to depression, putting one in a lonely, dangerous zone. I have heard about people suffering from depression wanting to take their own lives. Start eating healthy today and stop procrastinating, for procrastination is a precursor to failure. Stop making excuses. Change your eating pattern today.

Exercise sharpens the mind and keeps you alert. It helps with good posture, enhances self-confidence, and builds internal energy, assisting you in properly managing the daily demands of life. It builds strength, tones muscles, enhances vitality, and promotes positive energy. It relieves stress while improving general well-being. A person who exercises regularly has more energy reserves than someone who doesn't. Think about it. If you don't have energy, you feel tired and fatigued. If you don't eat well and exercise, your body may be prone to diseases. Someone who is in better physical health and sharp may be hired before someone who is sluggish. Being overweight leads to under conditioning of the body. Remember, keeping fit need not be frustrating; a few lifestyle changes can be helpful in weight management.

Every year, I get bombarded with interesting New Year's resolutions from my clients, 90 percent of which center on losing weight. Yet none of them is able to keep to his or her resolution throughout the whole year. Making a resolution is no doubt a laudable effort, but often we fail halfway through. The easiest way to keep resolutions is to work on achieving them piecemeal. It does not matter how many resources you have available to work with. Once you start, the universe steps in with the tools you need to support you in achieving your desired goals. Stop thinking of the reasons you will fail in your resolutions. Think of the reasons you must succeed. Do something daily toward achieving your goal. I place all my written goals inside my morning devotional prayer book so that I see them when I start the day. This works wonders. Remember that not all your goals are reachable, but most times they are. Once you achieve, please celebrate. It is a blessing to be excited, so get excited even when nothing is exciting you. It is good for your well-being. I have had a friend ask several times why I always seem excited. My answer: because I am always excited—I am a professional excitement expert.

Once you achieve a feat, cross it off and move on to the next goal. There is power in seeing your tasks accomplished and crossed off on your list. It assures you that you're making progress. The key is that you must do something on daily basis. I made sure I wrote something every day in my manuscript when I was working on the book you are now reading. Not only did that make me stay on track, but it also put me in the right frame of mind to see my goal accomplished.

Small steps taken strategically and regularly add up to gigantic steps that can change your life forever. Try these tips to see negatives gradually become positives, your movement gradually shifting toward success, and your goals gradually becoming achieved. I have always asked God to give me the desires of my heart in a society where I can reach for my dreams to be a blessing to humankind. I applied these principles step by step, prayed daily, and gave thanks in advance, and when God answered my prayers, I had no option but to find a way to give back to the world. This book is one of the by-products of that resolution. You can do same by taking small steps today to realize your big dreams.

The tips on these pages have proven very useful to all those who have connected with them. No matter your resolution—whether it is to lose weight, earn some college credits, or fly to space—the important thing is to incorporate mental energy into your acts. Just like potential energy, mechanical energy, or kinetic energy, there is also mental energy. Mental energy is the energy that fires when we think, the energy that processes our thoughts and sets great ideas and information in motion. It's a powerful energy in the universe available to champions who want to create powerful things. Every creative achievement originates in the brain, the seat of mental energy. Just as the arms have the biceps muscles and the legs have the quadriceps muscles, the brain has muscles, too. The first step to success is in learning how to exercise the mental muscles, the muscles that fire your brain to produce creative thoughts. Think of it this way: when you exercise your arm muscles by lifting weights, you build strength, develop muscle mass, increase the muscle fibers, and bulk and tone up. The same principle applies to mental muscles. When you exercise your mental muscles, you give energy to your willpower and strength to your thoughts.

Without willpower every New Year's resolution is useless and most times becomes ineffective by the first quarter of the year. How can you give juice to your willpower? First, limit your use of electronic gadgets, and think with your brain instead. We live today in a world saturated with cell phones, televisions, iPods, computers, iPads, calculators, and other electronic gadgets that seem to make life faster but in essence slow us down. We have outsourced the use of our brains to most of these gadgets and have disregarded the use of mental energy to solve simple but challenging problems. Limiting the use of these gadgets puts the brain in an active, creative state to better think about how you can solve problems to improve your life. No doubt these gadgets come in handy, but they also negate the use of the power of your brain cells.

Consuming good food improves willpower as well. Nuts are loaded with substances that improve brain health. Eating right means eating the right amount of vegetables, oils, fiber, complex carbohydrates, fruits, nuts, and protein and avoiding foods loaded with useless sugars that weaken the immune system, lead to weight gain, impair liver function, increase blood glucose levels, and can predispose the body to adult-onset diabetes. Learn to read food labels to make better buying choices. Avoid foods that contain high fructose corn syrup and cheap additive products that sweeten foods, with names like maltose, corn syrup, high fructose, or juice concentrate. These products should be limited in your diet because they overwork the pancreas, the organ that produces insulin, the substance that regulates blood sugar in your body. One very important habit is eating regular but small meals to avoid low blood sugar. Low blood sugar can cause fatigue, mood changes, excessive hunger, shaking, fainting or even make you feel disoriented. It can also cause difficulty in concentration. Don't wait until you're very hungry or starving to eat. Studies have shown that people tend to snack and eat more junk food when their blood glucose is very low because such a level makes it more difficult to control eating impulses. Although food is necessary and vital for human functioning, you should not forget the benefits of moderated eating.

Never underrate the power of exercise. You don't have to debate whether to exercise regularly or not; make exercising an automatic and enjoyable part of your lifestyle. Debating about exercising just takes a toll on your mental energy. It is never too late to start. The easiest way to start is to exercise as soon as you wake up in the morning. Start with stretching while still in bed. Even cats and dogs stretch when they first wake up. Isn't that too cool? Then take ten deep breaths to improve lung perfusion. When you get out of bed, do a few stretches coupled with a few push-ups on the floor. Starting with stretching first thing in the morning conditions the mind to kick off the day with exercise before daily distractions begin. Over time you'll stick to the routine. As you progress you can join a gym and engage in more powerful training with resistance equipment, depending on your goals. Morning exercise should be regular before starting the day. Why? It recharges your whole body and keeps you in shape and puts you in the mind-set to approach the day with vigor.

Playing back ground music during exercise increases the desire to work harder. Music keeps you happy, and listening while working out gives you that feel-good energy needed for maximum productivity throughout the day. You can sing along if you know the lyrics. That's even more fun. You can never go wrong with singing your favorite song while working out. By doing so, you build extra strength in your lungs as you gasp for air to maintain your rhythm and pace, thereby increasing your energy level and strength. You will think better, be more mentally alert, and make better-informed decisions.

Oftentimes in my public engagements, I get lots of questions centered on how to improve the drive and desire to exercise. In my answers I make my audience understand that in order to achieve anything in life, one must be determined. This means you must be ready to push hard and never give up. No matter how tough things may seem now or how frustrated you feel in starting, I empower you to just keep pushing forward. Sometimes you just want to throw in the towel. Don't. When things get tough, you must match the brutal force with an equal or higher progressive toughness and push past the challenge. One thing is clear: if you're willing to push a little harder, you'll see yourself driving forward to victory across the finish line, a stage decorated only for the tough and daring, the determined champions.

POWER CORNER

Exercise improves strength, relieves stress, and calms the body. Resolve to get some today, and moving forward, your body will always thank you.

THE POWER OF GIVING: OPENING DOORS FOR ABUNDANCE

GIVING IS THE PRACTICE OF LENDING assistance, an act that creates a feeling of equality, love, and oneness. Simple acts of giving cause smiles, improve health, and induce happiness. Giving is one of the easiest ways to be happy. Giving is medicine to the body that soothes the heart and nourishes the soul; the experience brings joy, success, and good things. Giving is a sign of nobility that warms and touches the deepest part of the heart.

Giving is about touching lives, making someone smile, and lending hope to others. Giving affects both the giver and the receiver and has been proven to enhance immunity. It creates an atmosphere of good feeling, producing the secretion of feel-good hormones into the system. I try to never miss any opportunity to give to those who desperately need my services, and I have benefitted immensely from the blessings of giving.

Some time ago, a young girl who worked at the local supermarket and had always greeted me politely and made pleasant jokes whenever I shopped was walking in the very cold winter weather to work. I had driven past her, but seeing her in my rearview mirror, I pulled over and waited until she got to me. I asked if she needed a ride, and without hesitation she jumped into the car. It was not a coincidence that I had taken the same route in my car. You see, not too long ago following my immigration to the United States, I myself was walking to work. I fell many times in the slippery, snowy road, and I appreciated it when someone who knew me was pleasant enough to offer me a ride to save me from the freezing cold. I wanted to extend to her the same courtesy I occasionally received and greatly appreciated.

When we got to her workplace, I grabbed a bottle of water from my car and some money from my wallet and gave them to her. I figured that if she did not have the money to pay for a taxi to work or to take the bus, she probably didn't have money to pay her way home. I told her the money might come in handy when she punched out of work later. She was extremely grateful and said it was the nicest thing anyone had done for her all week. I was sad that she had already been walking for about twenty minutes and was very tired and cold. But I was very pleased to have had the opportunity and privilege to be in a position to give. Not only was I kind to her, but the act humbled me. It made me feel fantastic on the inside and made my heart warm and fuzzy.

Giving is the best exercise you can give to your heart. If you want your heart to feel happier, give. If you want to build equity in your emotional bank, give more frequently. Giving is best appreciated when it is from the heart, without selfish intentions. The best is giving without expecting anything in return, especially to those who may not be able to repay you. Sometimes we give and expect honor in return. That is wrong. A simple thank-you means a lot. That's all you need, nothing more. Your gifts may not be celebrated. Your acts may not be recognized. Your charity may not be appreciated. But one thing is clear: it will not go unrewarded. Someone somewhere is watching what, how, and where you give. He is keeping records and will reward you in due time. God has already planned what you will give and strategically puts that in your giving bank. He already knows whom you will give to, and he positions them for you. Opportunities for giving do not happen by coincidence. He plans them. You are only running his errand. So give with excitement, especially when you give without expecting material gratification. No matter your age, there is always something you can give. God never forgets that you blessed the people he positioned in your path. He blessed you to bless others. So give with joy. The more you give, the more you receive. It is a natural law of the universe.

What you give doesn't have to have material or monetary value. Recall what Peter gave to the lame man: "Silver or gold I do not have, but what I have I'll give. I command you to stand up and walk." Peter did not give money or any tangible thing. He gave what he had at the time. He gave hope, energy, and love. He gave healing. Your faith may not be as strong as Peter's to heal, but you can always give something, no matter how small, to someone who desperately needs it. As soon as the lame man received strength in his muscles and was able to walk again, he jumped up and started rejoicing and praising God. That is the power of gratitude. It can make you do unimaginable things in unusual places. You can only imagine how Peter felt in his heart, having orchestrated this miraculous act. I believe his heart felt very warm.

When you give, you not only add to people's comfort, but you also sow seeds in their lives. You are sowing everlasting seeds in God's vineyard. You're blessing his people. If you learn to give your best services to people who need them the most without seeking gratification, God will also sow seeds in your life and give you his best. He will expand your life beyond your wildest imagination and bless you in measures that will overwhelm you.

Oprah Winfrey, in one of many giving exercises, built the one-of-a-kind Oprah Winfrey Leadership Academy for Girls near Johannesburg, South Africa. Her aim was to give poor but smart young South African women golden opportunities for academic excellence. Not only is the school creating future academicians, but it is also championing leaders of South Africa's tomorrow. Those girls were the first South Africans born around the time the late Nelson Mandela was released from prison. They never experienced apartheid. Some of the first graduating students are now engaging their lives positively and living their dreams in America and the world over.

But you don't have to build a school in South Africa or champion a movement for the homeless in England to be a giver. You can always give something—on the job, in school, at your church, or in your local community. You can even give while driving by letting two or more people pull in front of you. If you're a senior, you can give wisdom to the younger generation. You can buy your coworker a healthy snack on your way back from lunch. You can volunteer at your local library. If you're blessed with inspiration, you can give a pro bono speech to empower others. You can spare that homeless guy around the corner some change for his next meal. You can visit your neighbors who are in need, spend time with them, and have a full conversation with them. You can pour out your heart in listening to them and their life stories, experiences, and challenges. You can offer ideas when solicited on ways to improving their lives. Guess what? You have no idea how much you will be appreciated and how much you can learn from others. You will always be blessed immensely for the seeds you sow in the lives of people you encounter on a daily basis. No matter how old or young you are, there is always something you can give to change someone else's life.

Do not be stingy with your blessings. You're blessed to bless others. I advise you to give something on daily a basis as a form of gratitude for all your blessings. See the world as a place where your impact must be felt, where your personality must be seen, and where you must give something to change someone else's life. Giving brings joy. If you want to be happy, try to give often. Giving expands your wealth and attracts blessings. I have seen it work massively in my life and in others' lives, and it can work for you. Find something to give—even if it's just a smile—and assess how you feel afterward. The more you give, the happier you will be; over time your life will be full of happiness, and you will attract positive forces from the universe to create more things to be grateful for. You will never lack when you form the habit of giving. It is a practical law.

I think my genes have predisposed me to giving. A few years ago, I was in Nigeria, West Africa, my home country, on a short vacation. Temperatures were very high, as usual, and as I sat in a roadside restaurant to have a bottle of water to cool off, a man walked up to me, looking hungry. He asked if he could get twenty naira from me, which amounted to less than twenty cents of US currency then. I thought that if he was begging for just twenty cents, he probably didn't have the means to eat a decent meal. Without thinking, I asked if he had eaten, and as I suspected, he hadn't. I asked that he be fed with any menu of his choice. He ate, and we talked briefly. He sounded very polished and likely was very smart. You see, from time to time, people go through challenging situations that degrade their social status. As he left I gave him some money when he shook my hand. He opened his hand, saw the money, and turned back for a hug with an expression and posture of happiness and gratitude, having realized I'd given him over one hundred times what he asked for. I felt very happy deep down in my heart that I could support his needs. I was excited that I could deposit something into his life. I felt honored with his presence and for his having presented me with the opportunity to meet his demands.

One thing I have realized in my life is that giving creates channels for gratitude and as such ignites the magnifying effect of a grateful heart. When you give something, you demonstrate that you are happy to give and are grateful for what you have. You don't have to have a reason to give or predict how your gift will be utilized. Just give, forget the gift and move on while expecting the next giving opportunity. You'll definitely be rewarded. When you create time to cultivate the vineyard of those who desperately need your services, God will cultivate your farms, and you'll reap abundant harvest in due time. It is a natural law that still stands for those who practice it. Get out of your territory today and do some random acts of giving, and watch how you feel. I know you will feel very good. When you constantly perform good deeds, focusing more on what will benefit others; over time you create a movement for a moral code of conduct.

Giving complements gratitude. When you are grateful, your life radiates positivity at all times because you can always find something to be happy for and you'll receive more things to be grateful for. Gratitude is a force that attracts things to you as you radiate more of it. It is a powerful universal magnetic force. It is a global phenomenon and is always in motion. Gratitude reorganizes, rearranges, and reforms our moral standards. It shapes our lives and creates momentum for abundance. I have seen it work in my own life and in the lives of others, and it will work in yours if you believe and apply the principles. What kind of gift makes you feel loved? As humans, we all want to receive a gift motivated by love and not by egoistic showmanship or by a sense of duty or obligation. When we give, our motive is very important, and it matters so much to God. Recall what motivated Paul in 2 Corinthians 9:7: "Every man according as he purposes in his heart, so let him give; not grudgingly, or of necessity; for God loves a cheerful giver."

This is a great message from Paul. But why? Because Paul wanted to encourage the Corinthian Christians to support the charity work of their less privileged fellow brethren in the land of Judea. Just as he mandated the Corinthians, Paul wants us to give as we desire in our hearts. In essence we must not give under duress. We should give because we want to give, not because someone else wants us to give. No one wants to receive a gift from a mandated giver. I certainly don't. When you want to give, give with joy, love, and humility. In giving our time, encouragement, energy, or love, we must do so out of the abundance and generosity of our hearts. I have realized that happiness is a by-product of giving. Giving with joy always shows in the life of the giver, especially when you give to the less fortunate.

Let me explain how this can work in your life. When you believe in something with all your heart, that same thing manifests in your life. When you receive blessings and are grateful for them and give willingly to others who need them, you will surely receive more things to be grateful for. To receive you must inject faith into your thoughts. Positive thoughts you hold in high esteem manifest in your life as blessings. But for this to work, you must have a passion for the feelings. You must act with all your emotional energy—your heart, your love, and total sincerity. The action component is very important, for there is never a reaction without an action. In fact, action is the very most important part of creation. The size of the action does not matter. Action is action. Success depends on what small actions you're taking now. There must be some positive actions going on at all times in your life. All universal blessings enhance our growth. Every tool we need is strategically deposited in the universe. Your role is to apply the tools. A little touch of class, variety, and deviation from the norm creates unexpected results, and when you see results, you must step up your game to move to the next level. There is no limit to the heights you can reach. You are destined to be successful, but you must connect with the game you're playing because life itself is a big game. Get serious today to be linked to your greater tomorrow. You have the divine energy and the ability to do great things. So feel it, and make it happen. You'll see things change. I can assure you that things will positively shift in your direction. Remember as you receive to be grateful. It is a very good feeling to be grateful. Say aloud the things you're grateful for, and you'll receive more. It is good for your heart, your immunity, and your whole being.

POWER CORNER

You have the divine energy and the ability to do great things. There is no cap on how much you can grow and achieve here. Start something new today, and you'll be amazed by your latent possibilities.

THE POWER OF HUMILITY: A KEY TO SUCCESS

HUMILITY MEANS ACTING AND BEING MODEST. Humility is living a simple life, not feeling superior to others, and keeping a low profile. Humility is maintaining who we truly are, our worth, and our personality without pride or arrogance. You can—and should—be humble yet confident. Humility means being very fair to others around you and doing to others as you would have them do to you. It allows others to discover our powerful inner nature. Humility does not stop you from pursuing your dreams; it enhances your personality as you create the drive for success. It is an attribute that you can choose for yourself, a positive virtue that enhances success, creates avenues for personal growth, and opens doors to opportunities. Humility makes you have compassion for the homeless guy on the street corner. Humility is lending a helping hand to a stranger, irrespective of your status or academic background. There is always a spot of one's life that has the humble nature inscribed in it. But oftentimes people get so carried away with their success that they lose sight of their inner humble nature. Humility can open up a flood of possibilities and great opportunities. And put in a simple language, "The lord takes pleasure in his people; he honors the humble with victory" (Psalm 149:4).

Humility is a choice. Choosing humility means we are open-minded. Encouraging the practice of humility in our lives, our homes, and our jobs and to anyone we meet opens doors for personal growth.

It improves relationships, enhances lives, and encourages openness of mind, and it can be a positive force in building self-confidence. With a confident spirit, you can take any risk, go places, and meet new people and as such open windows of opportunity for progress. Once those opportunities are available, you have to connect with them and make maximum use of their availability. Some opportunities are easy to follow up on while some are difficult and require perseverance and determination to pull through. Following through may require your willingness to explore beyond safe borders. As you do you'll learn more and connect with more people and more golden opportunities. Sometimes you need to be in a never-quitting attitude to move forward, and when you push with a combination of perseverance and a humble belief in yourself and in your plan, you create the channel for progress. Once you start out on the road, which could be smooth or rough, you gain experience as you pilot your course and gain more confidence as you progress.

As you progress, you speak energy-loaded words like, "I can do this," "I am ready for this," and "I have everything it takes to do this" and repeat them several times a day. Even when you hit a snag, which is part of the process, you reenergize your thoughts and set the bar a little higher and then move on to the next level. But to be able to have this type of mind-set, you have to be humble. You have to be able to respect every person, every challenge, and every thought that you perceive as you pilot your projects. If you're humble, you will notice the help and solutions that pop up as you progress. Humility sharpens your belief in yourself and opens up opportunities for growth.

I learned a lot about humility from the birth of Jesus Christ. Consider the following, from Luke 2:7–8: "And she gave birth to her firstborn son and wrapped him in swaddling clothes and laid him in a manger; because there was no room for them in the inn. And in the same region there were shepherds out in the field, keeping watch over their flock by night." The powerful lesson to be learned from this passage is simply the principle of humility. In simple language, it teaches us that powerful things can come from humble starts. Remember where this child was born—in a manger. History informs us of what this same child did in his lifetime and of his impact on humanity, especially within the Christian belief system. Every human being is born the same—ordinary, wrapped in simple clothes, but possessing great potential.

Oftentimes as we grow older, we shortchange ourselves, lower our bars, and limit our human capabilities. We limit our rise to glory because we feel too ordinary. Intimated by the forces of life or by the dehumanizing gymnastics of others around us, we limit our chances of doing better. We fail to see that many good things can emanate from humble beginnings. Being wrapped in a cloth does not mean you're ordinary or worthless. That humble beginning can be the tonic that stimulates you to expand your drive for growth. Even if life has unleashed devastating blows on you, you can still change your world and make it big. Your humble beginnings should be the catalyst needed to fire on, break through, and succeed.

I came from a tough background, a well-disciplined culture in which every parent in the village automatically became my parent by communal induction, a society that imparted unlimited rectitude in every aspect of life. My strict parents lived an average but simple life. There were no cell phones then. They could not afford a car, and life was a little rough, but I was never disturbed or limited by these temporary deficiencies. Rather, I saw them as a stepping-stone to success. Humility was the order of the day. My late mother would always stress the importance of humility. Immigrating to America created a massive avenue of golden opportunities for me to practice the wealth of knowledge I received from this humble society, and I will forever remain grateful that I am part of the most powerful country in the world and, to my credit, that I have written and authored two books, including The Power to Excel: Reaching for Your Best and the one you are reading. I am still expanding my abilities for living bigger dreams.

If you live a life of humility, you will be respected and liked. People will present you with opportunities to meet more people wanting to associate with you to help you grow. I always try to find a way to help others. I take more time in assisting others. I've realized that the more I take responsibility for others, the more value I add to my existence on earth. Assuming responsibility motivates me to take on the next challenge and involve different people to assist, and most times I get positive results.

Humility allows you to maintain your pride while still being you and it can be practiced in numerous ways. The person who volunteers to clean up the office or assist others in moving things around is displaying humility. So too is the staff member who offers his time to assist in training new employees. The supervisor who offers to help you complete some of your work while you are tied up in some other things is displaying humility. I read of a successful business tycoon in Africa who anonymously sponsors poor but brilliant students so that they can attend various colleges worldwide. When we do things from a humble perspective, we attract people; we deposit a feeling of connection in people's hearts and get noticed. Humility makes us swallow our pride to immerse ourselves deeply in the service of others. We learn more in being humble, and we gain more because people open up their hearts to support us. When we put others in the limelight and subject ourselves to the enclave of our humble nature, they will move to do things in our behalf. There are simple ways to learn how to be humble. Allowing others to share their views is a sign of humility. It tells them that they are relevant and important in your presence. Sharing success stories with others is also a simple practice of humility. I have always appreciated people around me and made it an obligation to give credit when earned. Humility improves relationships. It creates a channel for bonding and allows us to leave indelible marks on people's lives. It has opened massive doors for me.

It's always gratifying to create a good impression of oneself with humility. Any trait you display at first impression will be carried over to future encounters, so it becomes imperative that you give a positive impression when meeting people for the first time. If you meet them again and remember to greet them by their first names, they'll connect better with you. If you offer assistance to people when you can and keep your promises to them, they'll feel comfortable working with you. That's humility in action. Good association is very important. When you find common ground with people, it becomes very easy to create a bond. Such a bond ultimately develops into a trusting friendship and opens doors for peaceful coexistence. Remember, you're identified with your associations. Humans all over the world have social needs, but your contributions to a group will determine the benefits you derive. If you want people to support you, you must genuinely support them. We all have great plans, but we have to be very careful how we disclose them to some of the people around us, including our friends, family, neighbors, or even acquaintances, for some can discourage us out of our plans and kill our dreams. My stand is this: if you believe in your ideas and know they will positively affect your life, society, and the world, just turn deaf ears on all the distractions and do your thing. In order to get results, you must develop a thick skin against rubbish. I have learned to have zero tolerance for nonsense and never condone anyone who comes to me with garbage thoughts.

Goodwill enhances humility. Genuine goodwill unto others creates an atmosphere of peace and makes people want to be around you. This involves saying positive things, expressing your excitement when others succeed, and showing genuine consolation if they fail. Showing goodwill builds equity in people's emotional bank. You must be there for people in order to be liked and trusted. When people trust you, they're more likely to do things for you when you need their services. If your work ethic is poor and you can't support others happily and timely with your blessings of creativity, you'll have serious problems with trust. Everything we learn on earth is a form of education. But understand that formal education is not life—being educated does not make you an automatic success. Rather, education is the master key to unlocking the golden doors of success. The fact that you completed high school, graduated from college with double master's degrees in physics and astronomy, and hold a PhD in nuclear medicine does not mean you'll be successful and fulfilled. The key is to use the knowledge acquired from formal education to unleash your innate potential to create a great life and achieve the things you want to accomplish with a view to being happy while positively affecting others on your way. Education is great, but talent is greater. Talent plus vision and passion is what makes you stand out from the crowd.

Education + Talent + Vision + Passion = Ingenuity

Understand that you are not reinventing the wheel. You aren't expected to travel to every nook and cranny of the world to make an impact. But you can always make a little difference that benefits the world. You're created with elegance and purpose, and you must strive to fulfill that purpose. You must be alert so that you can listen and act when called upon. When God ordered Moses to speak, Moses doubted his innate powers, saying he was not eloquently endowed. But he was reminded that he already had the skills to obey and act. As soon as he believed and moved with faith, God rearranged his verbal commands, and he spoke with great charisma. God does not mince words. His mandate is firm and direct. But you must be determined and confident to move with poise and execute whatever project he places in your path. You can ignore your ideas, refuse to yield to your annoying enemies, but don't block your auditory canals when God speaks, asking you to make a move. Listen when he speaks, move, and take calculated risks. You must constantly evolve by trying new things, no matter the challenges, to make an impact in the annals of history. Get your name out there, and design yourself on the world map. The world soccer pitch is level for everyone, but you must play your game with skill to be able to score that golden goal that initiates celebration. We are all blessed with a gift of twenty four hours in a day. Use yours wisely. Add some poise, confidence, and a few deviations from the usual way you do things. It may sound tough, but you can do it. In this modern era of beautiful creations, the only way to fail is to not try, and the reason you have crashed is that you have not tried something new.

POWER CORNER

Try something new, no matter the challenges. Believe wholeheartedly to achieve, and make an impact to stamp your foothold in the annals of history. You'll be celebrated wherever you go. You'll feel good both on the inside and outside.

THE POWER OF LOVE: IT CONQUERS EVERYTHING

LOVE HAS BEEN PRACTICED SINCE THE beginning of life. Love is practiced by people in every part of the world. Love has been taught in schools, in churches, in colleges, and in families. As a child I would often tell my mother how much I loved her. I may not have understood the real meaning of love then, but it was something I needed no formal education to express. It was a feeling that came from my heart with great humility, and I meant it each time I said it. It was part and parcel of my life, and I continued that same tradition until she passed on. Even after her death, I always remind myself how much I loved her.

Love is patient and kind, never proud or rude. Love is powerful, potent, and healing. It is not physically visible to the naked eye, but it is always in motion with a dynamic force. It is one of the greatest powers in the universe. It is a moving force, a healing word, a function of charity. To offer charity there must be love in the giver's heart. Love expresses affection and care even when you don't feel like it. When you show compassion for others, you are giving love. Love comes from the heart. How do you give from the heart? By thinking of others as much as you think of yourself. By thinking less of ourselves, we channel some love to others, increasing the power of love in us and activating its potency to create change. Love creates riches, especially when you touch others with your wealth of love. True riches come from a little touch of love. When you show love, you show affection and generosity, and you attract the same to yourself. When you show affection for others, you attract the same to yourself. If you care about people, you care about yourself, too. Love means kindness, generosity, and tolerance.

As humans, we all have the potential to reflect God's rare personality traits of care, love, compassion, justice, peace, and wisdom. When we act out of love, we become like God and practice his principles. God created us with love and wants us to practice it. He created the universe with love and wants us to enjoy it. His will for us is magnificent. The more we love and care for people as God directs, the more we live according to his commands. By doing so we attract much love, joy, abundance, inner peace, and contentment, and we live happier. Resonating these qualities in your heart creates an avenue for rapid growth, and as you grow you bring more good things to yourself; you attract people from whom you can learn and with whom you can share ideas, two precursors to success.

As a sophomore in a physics class in the university, I studied some of the forces and laws in the universe. We studied the force of gravity and learned the laws of electromagnetism, the law of relativity, Ohm's law, Avogadro's law, the law of partial pressure, Newton's laws of motion, the ideal gas laws, the law of thermodynamics, and the law of equilibrium, to mention but a few. We studied very hard, day and night, burning the midnight candles. We made sacrifices, memorized these laws, and reproduced them to our professors and thus passed the examinations and moved on to the next semester. But as we passed more examinations, moved on to the next class, graduated from college, and progressed further, we never thought of or studied the law of love as a powerful law of the universe. With love, God created the entire universe and decorated it with abundant resources to enhance our lives. When you critically examine the beauty of human creation—the birds, the oceans, the trees, the earth, the air we breathe, water, food, people, animals, the moon, the sky, the planets, the stars, and sea creatures—you'll see amazement. God created and endowed us with the knowledge to invent things that enhance our lives: cars, roads, railways, iPhones, electric stoves, homes, and so many great ventures emanating from the creativity of the human mind. They're all God's creations, crafted with love. If God created the universe with love that means everything in the universe emits love. So if you love God's creations, you love him and you're a product of his creation. He puts dreams in your heart and gives you the tools to work with to make those dreams a reality.

In my motivational speeches, I remind people that every great achievement began with a small dream. It could be a dream you had in your living room, while driving, while asleep, in school, at the supermarket, or even in prison. We all have the freedom to dream, and every dream has potential. Any dream can grow if fed the right fuel. Your dreams can be small or big—it doesn't matter. What matters is that the universe is big, and God—who is bigger—positioned the universe to your advantage, if only you're willing to dream. So let your mind wander freely with dreams. You must love your dream. The size of your dream has no relationship to others, their approval, or your current status. Remember, there is no cap on how much you can dream. Even if you are homeless, unemployed, unmarried, separated, divorced, angry, frustrated, unattached, depressed, childless, or hopeless, your dream should not be influenced by circumstances. God is aware that you are in existence and will align you with your dream to bring it to fruition. Motivate yourself to doing something to bring your dreams to reality. If one dream fails, analyze it. Discover what went wrong, and then tighten the loose nuts right away. At times you may need to start afresh with a new dream. Are you dreaming big today? If yes, fine. If no, why not? If you're not dreaming, you're denying yourself the free right of creativity. You're missing opportunities and God's abundant blessings. Dream something today to change something tomorrow.

Bill Gates had a dream. Initially, it may have seemed small, but he had a dream, period. He dreamed of a world where every family would have a simple device for reaching out. Today his dream is changing lives worldwide. Mark Zuckerberg had a dream of creating a forum for people to reconnect with lost contacts, hence the birth of Facebook. The late Nelson Mandela dreamed of a free South Africa. Mother Theresa dreamed of using compassion to heal souls. When the late Steve Jobs dreamed of Apple Computer Inc., he may not have believed he would change the world. It was just a dream. Today his dream of putting computers in people's palms is a global phenomenon. I benefit massively from that fact, and you can, too. Remember, Jobs was in his twenties when he dreamed; he had neither a business background nor expertise. He was just an ordinary guy who believed in enhancing his life to bring global blessings to humanity. These people dreamed but applied the most important factor—action. They were dedicated and focused; they believed in their dreams and worked consistently to actualize them. They gave hope, time, energy, attention, and possibly prayer for their dreams to explode, and they did.

I had a dream to immigrate, to live and work in the United States, and it came true. I had a dream to give back to my community, and it came true. I had a dream to become an author, and this book is one of the by-products of that dream. I had a dream of becoming a successful motivational speaker, and that, too, came to pass. Your dreams don't have to mimic mine. Dream your own dream. You can dream in the United Kingdom, Zambia, the United States, Tonga, Denmark, Jamaica, Switzerland, Laos, Swaziland, Japan, Burkina Faso, Honduras, China, Australia, and Mexico. You can dream in the Island of Seychelles in

Africa. You can dream anywhere on earth, even in the forest. But when you dream, give your dream some energy. Talk to your dream. If you take action, I can assure you that it won't be long before you'll be coasting to the finish line with joy. If you're willing to change your thinking, you can create anything you focus on. So have a vision and a passion, invest energy and time, and you'll see things shift in your favor.

God gave you the beautiful gift of love and passion, but you must use it well to attract beautiful things. God gave Daniel the gift of interpreting dreams, Peter the gift of healing, and Elisha the gift of prophesies. No matter where you are, no matter your academic background or your financial status, you are created with an abundance of resources to succeed. Oftentimes the road is bumpy. Yes, we make mistakes because no one is infallible. The key is this: avoid dwelling on your failures. Instead, learn from your mistakes, make adjustments, incorporate every positive pronouncement to sharpen your mental recovery, and then move on. Declare positive things to restore your self-esteem.

Your perception of yourself determines your productivity. You must love yourself. On a self-esteem scale with a maximum score of fourteen, if your self-esteem is five or less, you must work hard to push it up to ten or twelve to be able to operate powerfully. Your life is seriously influenced by how you feel. Do you have an inferiority complex? If you believe everything people tell you, you have an esteem issue and may have a serious problem, one that can be dangerously retrogressive. Hanging around positive people will help build your self-esteem. Some people will empower you, some will frustrate your actions, and some will totally avoid you because you're doing better than they are. Stick with those who believe in you and your ideals and want you to succeed. Bond with those who spend their time motivating you to be the best. Pay no attention to people's negative thoughts of you as long as you're doing the right thing. Pay more attention to what you think of yourself and how you'll progress by being productive with a zeal for achieving what you set your mind on.

To change your life, you must love yourself, change your perception, believe in yourself, and appreciate yourself. Cheer yourself on, and when you achieve something, no matter how small, congratulate yourself even if no one else does so. I salute God, give thanks, and do a quick dance at every breakthrough. It empowers me. Discover what works for you. Appreciate your success, but genuinely congratulate others as well. Don't be stingy with your compliments. When you love and rejoice with others, the same comes right back to you. But in complimenting others, avoid comparisons. This is a common mistake. There is no need to be unnecessarily competitive. It's OK to compete with yourself. Everyone on earth is born to run his or her individual marathon. But comparing yourself to others creates a false picture that you're not doing well enough, which can bring sadness. Or it can make you arrogant, thinking you're ahead of others. That, too, is detrimental to your growth process and can be distracting. Rather than engaging in needless comparisons, get focused on your individual race and on things you can do to make a big impact in the society of which you're a part. Never limit yourself. If you stay on course, over time you'll look back and thank the universe and bless God for his mighty hands. Thanksgiving is a powerful force. Every day, I give thanks. As I see the sun rise, the cars rushing to beat the busy hour, the birds singing in synchrony, the wind blowing and children walking to nearby schools, I thank God and salute his miracles.

Oftentimes we wish things for ourselves but never pull through. We feel like life has shut down, like we've hit a dead end or a closed door that will never open again. Understand this: when one door closes for good, another opens, but you must be alert to see and happily walk past that door with faith, a divine grace that makes the impossible very possible, an evidence of things you imagine by yourself for yourself. A closed door doesn't mean your dream has died. At times you need to alter things in order to break through the door. If you repeat the same pattern, you will meet the same roadblock. The key to open that new door lies within you, but you must identify and use it. If you're willing to press on, you'll eventually triumph.

Never give up on your dream; focus on getting to your destination. Most people chicken out when their dreams die. Rather than dreaming another dream, they resign themselves to fate, and throw pity parties to celebrate their failure. I feel very sorry for those who give up on a task because it's too hard. They say, "The task is very hard," "I don't have the resources," "I don't think I can pull through," or "I will fail if I try." So what? You can do it. You can. Never stop because you hit a roadblock. I have learned to thank God for closed doors; I glorify him for the road-blocks. You must understand that if God wants you to tread that path, nobody on this earth can stop you. He closes doors for his own reasons, and he will always open another one for you. Don't let anything stop you from discovering. The key to open that new door of greatness is in your dominant hand. Unlock that door, pass through it, and live your dream. Nobody can stop you but you, and you can only make it if you try.

POWER CORNER

The key to open that new door of greatness is in your dominant hand. Use it today to unlock your potential, pass through that door and live the life of your dreams.

THE POWER OF GRATITUDE: MAGNIFYING OUR BLESSINGS

GRATITUDE IS APPRECIATING WHAT YOU HAVE now, anything you had in the past, and that which you're expecting in future. Gratitude is being thankful even for the smallest things you receive on daily basis. It is appreciating yourself, your looks, your achievements and your beliefs. It is feeling good about your dreams. The power of gratitude is so huge that we often become overwhelmed with its benefits. Gratitude and love are interwoven. Oftentimes it is difficult to differentiate one from the other. Gratitude is choosing to love all things. Gratitude leads to feelings of love and appreciation while generating an aura of overwhelming happiness. It breeds generosity, which compels us to be more grateful and willing to share our blessings.

The human brain is very sensitive in picking up new signals. The more you think positive thoughts, the more your brain rewires to think only positive thoughts. This generates positive actions that metamorphose into achievements that keep you happy, making you even more grateful. The power of gratitude has always been with us. It began with life and is still in existence. How you think and feel affects your general well-being. Lack of gratitude breeds negativity, which initiates a chain reaction of depression, anger, fear, jealousy, and bitterness that can be poisonous and lead to failure. Gratitude generates positive feelings that benefit the heart. We all have a choice to feel good and be grateful or to be sad and ungrateful. The happier you are, the more grateful you are, so be grateful, be happy, feel good now, get excited, feel motivated to live the life you were created for. The more grateful you are, the more energized you will feel, and the more inspired you'll be.

Gratitude is saying "thank you" even when you don't feel like it. It shows that you truly appreciate things. It is a powerful force, one of the greatest energies in the universe. I have learned that each time I say "thank you" with all my heart, I receive something new. When you have any opportunity to change something, be it a friendship, your place of residence, your school, or your job, be grateful for that change. Change could be positive or negative, but either way, you'll learn something. Change can alter your mood; it can excite or depress you. Whichever is applicable, change must change you. Most times people fear change or get very nervous with the changes in their lives. I empower you to learn from change, make adjustments, and move on with your life. Change is a vital part that adds spice to life.

I have read of seemingly negative changes that produced positive results in people's lives. The apostle Paul made positive changes in his life during incarceration, writing almost half of the New Testament and becoming a product of change. His environment changed from one of freedom to one of restriction, but he was never deterred or depressed. He went to work and used the lessons learned from confinement to change something. Are you frightened by change? Don't be. It is a growth process that makes things better. It is sad that some people are scared of change. I empower you to drop that idea, change that mentality, step up your faith, banish fear, create a balance, and apply these forces to embrace the change. The change you experience daily is a way the universe communicates with you to keep track of, maintain, or rearrange your life. With the right mind-set, you can make a big change. So welcome change with love. There is no excuse for not accepting change. Excuses are poison, and they convince you to remain stagnant. They clog your flow of progress and negate your movement. So stop excuses now. It's a rare privilege to be in a position to be changed, so accept change with gratitude. Immigrating to the United States was an unprecedented change in my life. It was tough initially, but I embraced the change, made a few adjustments, focused my faith, believed more in myself and in God, and made positive moves toward living the new life of my dream. Things started shifting in my favor. I tripled my faith and created new things, and gradually my life took a great turn for the better. I am very grateful for change because it reminds me that I am making positive adjustments toward creating my dream life.

Gratitude is being thankful for your surroundings and your blessings. When that neighbor sends his or her greetings, be grateful—some neighbors can be apathetic or angry. When the gas attendant pumps gas into your car, be grateful—he is pumping life into your car. When the store manager forgives your declined debit card two days after pay day, be grateful for that kindness, which saved you public embarrassment. Students, be grateful for your teachers. If your coworker buys you a healthy snack on his way back from lunch, be grateful. If someone pulls out of the busy parking lot so that you can park, be grateful for the blessing. When people motivate you, be grateful you have encouraging people who are committed to seeing you succeed. Be grateful for humility, for love, for good energy. Be grateful for confidence.

If you're blessed with humility, be grateful, for humility is one of the greatest attributes of human character. Be grateful for all the experiences you've had. Be grateful for your parents, who nurtured you. Even if they are not living today, you can still be grateful that someone cared about you and are now watching over you. Be grateful for the shanty house you lived in before that state-of-the-art mansion you're living in now. Stop complaining about the high cost of things. Stop stressing about the rights that you are deprived of. Do not lose sight of the fact that at least you're alive. Be grateful for your health every single day. Nothing can buy or replace your health, the most powerful gift of humanity, your greatest asset. Be grateful for the teachers, schools, colleges, polytechnics, and universities that gave you an education and for the journals, newspapers, magazines, and news media that allow you to keep abreast with information. Be grateful for places of worship. Be grateful for people who make you happy, for they are the amazing angels who keep your heart warm. Be grateful for laughter, for humor and for peace. Be grateful for inspiration. Inspiration is everywhere even in your own living room, so be grateful everywhere. Be grateful for the power of love. Be grateful for opportunities to meet people who invest in your personal growth. Above all, be grateful to God, who places those people and opportunities in your path.

Be grateful for people who obeyed and respected you while under your supervision. They could've been disobedient and made your job a nightmare. When you fly, be grateful for the structural engineers that built the aircrafts, the stewards and stewardesses that served you in-flight food, and the pilots whose expertise flew you to your landing destination. Yes, you paid for those services, but it is still OK to express your feelings of gratitude. Be grateful for the street cleaners who keep our streets tidy, for the construction companies that repair our highways, for the seniors in your neighborhood for their wisdom and decades of loyal servitude to your community. Be grateful for the corner store that makes it easy for you to pick up those essential commodities when you need them most. Be grateful for money for your purchases; be grateful for the community and nature and the resources therein that make life beautiful. If you're a senior citizen, be grateful for your age—it is a blessing. Be grateful for the younger ones you inspire, for they constitute your blessings. If it weren't for them, you'd have no one to bless. Think about that. Young ones, be grateful for your parents and friends.

If you're in Africa, be grateful. If you're in Europe, be grateful. If you're in Asia or Oceania or South America, be grateful. Be grateful in New Zealand. Be grateful everywhere. Be grateful for music. I dance every day with excitement, even after my music ends, all in gratitude. There is always something to be grateful for. Can you see clearly with your prescription glasses? If yes, be grateful. Has your hair fallen out due to chemotherapy? Be grateful that you're still alive. Be grateful for electricity that lights up our world. Millions of people worldwide have no access to good food, electricity, good roads, and beautiful cars. They cannot afford brand-new clothes or even potable water, and yet they are very grateful. Many people living in highly developed countries have so much that they take many things for granted. That is unfair to humanity. If you take things for granted, please change that mind-set and give thanks daily for the abundance you have now. That is gratitude and it's the right thing to do.

If you cannot sleep after two o'clock in the morning, don't worry. Be grateful that you're alive and that you have a bed. A large percentage of the world's population has trouble sleeping well at night, so relax—you're not a lone ranger. Instead of complaining all night, be grateful, stay positive, and use that time to ask for guidance. Make up the sleep later in the day if you can. The truth is this: achievers are those who don't complain a lot. They try their hand at many projects without giving up. They plan at night when everything is calm and conducive for mental work and inspirational thinking. Above all, they are eternally grateful.

Be grateful for food and for water. Be grateful that you can drink, chew, and swallow without a nasogastric tube. Be grateful for e-mail, for text messages, for fax machines, for information technology, for social media, and for all the means we have to connect. Be grateful for people you meet daily, including those you inspire and those who empower you. Being thankful opens up channels for more beautiful things to flow into your life by creating avenues that help you succeed. When you're grateful, you focus on what is going well, on the things you have now, without dwelling on things you don't have or cannot afford. You feel more relaxed. Gratitude enhances contentment, sharpens alertness, improves health, boosts immunity, and increases your determination to work extra hard to acquire more good things to be grateful for. Gratitude makes you excited. How? Try this simple exercise to buttress my point. Raise your right hand into the air and give thanks aloud for just five big things you have, including the simple fact that you're alive. Now do the same thing for just three small things you're grateful for. How do you feel? I bet you feel great. Now make this a daily practice: study and keep a daily log of how you feel, and multiply that daily. Gratitude magnifies little things, and they become great things. It has created mighty miracles in my life, and I know it will do same in yours.

I know a young, beautiful woman who grew up under the love of her parents. Coming from humble beginnings, she lived a tough life, oftentimes with little or no food on the table. To compound matters, her father died shortly after she gained admission into the university. Despite these challenges, Esther was endowed with intelligence. Neither the death of her father nor the abject poverty she found herself in changed her level of gratitude. In fact, she often did a gratitude dance. She wrote on a piece of paper a long list of every single thing she was grateful for and recited the items daily like a poem. Oftentimes she composed and sang songs to express her gratitude. She was grateful for things such as seeing airplanes flying in the air. She defined her life with gratitude.

Over time she made good friends at the university. As they got to know her better, she was introduced to one friend's wealthy parents. That was the turning point in her life. As she told her story, not only did the parents understand and connect with her, but they placed her on scholarship. Her life changed. She became even more grateful, she rejoiced more, and she studied harder. Eventually she graduated from the university, and now she is living the dream. Esther is a living example of gratitude and someone I am very proud to call my friend.

The more grateful you are, the more blessed you feel, the more energy you radiate, and the more people will want to work with and assist you. People like to associate with happy people. Get excited with gratitude, and stop being sad for the things that are going wrong in your life. When life drops a bitter leaf into your mouth, rather than being angry or depressed, find something little that you're grateful for and then magnify that feeling a billion times. Watch as the situation reverses from depression to projection. As a practical exercise, let me narrow this down. Keep still and feel the things around you. Take a look at your surroundings. Feel the blessings, imagine the fact that you're alive, and take a deep breath. Still breathing, smile and declare, "I am alive and enjoying life." Understand that you have all the blessings you deserve because you can feel them now. Don't you feel better and more grateful? That is the multiplier effect of a grateful heart.

If you don't have to take a medication to sleep at night, be grateful. Even if you do, be grateful you can afford medications. If you don't have to force laughter, be grateful. If you have only three pairs of shoes but can't afford to buy ten extra pairs, be grateful. Some people have prosthetic legs and are forever grateful and taking big risks. For example, Nick Vujicic is an inspirational speaker who was born with a congenital condition called tetra-amelia syndrome, a rare disorder characterized by the absence of all four limbs. Though he may be disturbed by his challenges, he is always grateful. He is an author empowering people with amazing testimonies and a powerful story of faith and action; he is an inspiration with dynamic energy.

The key to enjoying life lies in daily gratitude. Remember to write a list of all the things you are grateful for; read them every morning with a grateful heart. This simple but powerful exercise gives you confidence by helping you maintain a positive attitude every day. Today declare to never let anything discourage you from being grateful. Grateful people are happier and more likely to live longer.

One great way to express gratitude is to volunteer. Your desire to serve others shows that you are grateful for your energy. Volunteering improves your mood by releasing so-called happy hormones into the body. Studies have shown that helping others without thoughts of gratification can relieve pain and improve well-being. Volunteering has no age limit. You can volunteer at eight or even eighty-eight. There is always something you can give to others in need. People with grateful hearts feel better emotionally because they find things daily to be happy for. Gratitude breeds happiness.

How can you be happy? If music makes you happy, play it. Dance every step, no matter where the beat takes you or when the music ends. What could be better than a song that refreshes your soul? It's up to you to act with love and gratitude. Love what you do. When you laugh, laugh with excitement. Laughter creates a feeling of peace in your heart, boosts immunity, and reveals your true personality, drawing people to you. No one wants to be around a sad person. I sure don't. In order to tap the benefits of happiness, you must love people. To imbibe the power of love means to love your enemies, and this means banishing from your mind animosity, insecurity, jealousy, and all forms of anger, which create bad blood and increase blood pressure by working up your system. These negative forces are your core enemies. It is a hard task for some people to love their enemies, and that is understandable. But it does not matter what wrong people did to you that may seem unforgivable. What matters is the magnitude of the burden of carrying the resentment with you, which prevents you from living a productive life full of peace, generosity, and excitement. Bitterness takes a toll on your spirituality and drains your mental energy. For the sake of life, forgive. But be careful: learn lessons from being hurt, and get wiser. Release the people who hurt you from your memory, wish them well, love them from a distance, and move on to the next level. At this level, you'll feel the peace of life emanate from within. Your brain will rewire itself to produce more positive feelings so that you can focus on what is important, keeping you renewed, energized, refreshed and thus making your life more exciting. The best way I avenge people who wrong me is to forgive them, move on with determination, and create a new movement. When I rebound with massive success, I watch them as they gnash their teeth in frustration. Forgiveness brings peace of mind and is the best revenge.

We all know that love is powerful. Having gratitude is having love, for one cannot radiate love without a grateful heart. It doesn't matter what you do, where you are, or who you are—the power of love is alive. It is the power through which we connect with people. Love changes circumstances, reduces stress, and is a ticket to beauty, energy, excitement, and peace of mind. Gratitude brings your mind into harmony with the creative energies of the universe. Gratitude guides your mind along the ways by which good things come to you because it keeps you appreciative of your own blessings while preventing you from competing with anyone. The path to happiness is not easy; it takes time to build. With a steady radiation of gratitude, you can start to be happier little by little and with time generate a force that can attract anything.

Oftentimes our gratitude isn't constant, and we're only grateful when we feel like being so. That's not good. We become so distracted by the events of daily life that we forget to be grateful. When that happens, the supply of what we can receive is limited, and we begin to think competitively and become frustrated and worried. We in effect shut off the gratitude channel, which stops the flow of good things into our lives, thus creating more bitterness. How can gratitude solve this? When you're in a constant state of gratitude, you focus on the things that are going well. You begin to see the universe as a supplier of all the tools you need to be successful. Being joyful has great benefits. God wants us to be abundantly happy and live freely with excitement, no matter the challenges. By doing so you align yourself with the evidence of faith, an unseen but positive force that surmounts all challenges. Let's move forward and be joyful, feel good on the inside, feel grateful and you can never go wrong with that.

If you concentrate only on the positive side of every situation, you will soon discover that your whole life will be radiating only positives, and you will be filled with gratitude, a feeling that keeps you energized at all times, a power food that nourishes the body. Life is what you put into it. If you desire to be happy and grateful, happiness and gratitude are yours. If you're sad all day, the negative forces will overpower you with more anger. You have been endowed with a drive to navigate out of difficulties. That's your divine destiny. But you've got to have the bounce-back mentality. There is always a way to see a seemingly negative situation with gratitude. For example, be grateful that you have life even though you may not have money for your next meal. Think about that.

Happiness is a natural medicine and is related to gratitude. You might say, "I am not always happy. I don't get easily excited. I don't smile or laugh much, and I don't feel good all the time." It is true we are created differently, but if you stand in joy, you stand strong, irrespective of what's going on in your life. Every human being is created with the power of creativity. The ability is already in you. Too many people don't recognize what God has deposited in them in terms of energy, power, force, and the drive to succeed. All of these are inside you, but they need nurturing. How do you nurture your gifts? By listening to your instincts as they direct you. It may not happen in a day, a month, or a year, but if you give it time, you'll discover and connect to your dreams. No dream is small or too big to be actualized. You have the power to train yourself to make things happen. To enjoy happiness, you must give happiness. Some people attempt to find happiness by forcing it, by partying or drinking excessively instead of giving happiness. But they will never find it until they give it. Happiness can heal, beautify, preserve, and enrich the soul, but it must be evenly distributed for you to tap into its power. If it is kept unshared, it has no potency. You must give to receive. It is like pouring baby powder on others without getting some of it. You know that's impossible.

Never allow the stressors of daily life to deny you of your free right of gratitude. Problems are part of life. You can always overcome challenges. It's all in your mind-set. Are you stressed out? Stress, an inevitable aspect of life, is manageable. There is good and bad stress, and what matters is how you react to the stress level. Bad stress is the stress you feel from overwhelming your body physically, emotionally, or mentally. Sometimes we overthink to solve all our problems in one shot. That puts the whole body under stress. An example of good stress is the tension you feel when friends are doing well in an event and you're excited for them and cheering them on to victory.

Are you feeling overstressed today? Then take a break. Play some good music, create humor, laugh with a friend who keeps your spirit light, and take thirty very deep breaths spaced throughout the day. If you engage in leisure activities, walk at the park, and enjoy the breeze, you'll feel relieved. Engage in cardiovascular exercise to keep your heart pumping and your blood flowing, hence lowering blood pressure and relieving stress. Dancing is a very good form of stress relief, too. I dance every day. Keep your body and soul together away from stress, for no one wants to be around a stressed-out person. Resolve today to look beyond stress and the frustrations of life to be happy. Be in an attitude of gratitude, and then ask God to refresh your life in the beautiful world he gave you. Then you can stretch your mind with a new vision.

POWER CORNER

Never allow the problems, challenges, pressures from people, and stresses of daily life to deny you of your free rights of gratitude, and joy. Instead, fill your heart with excitement. Choose to see beauty in all things, and immerse yourself in gratitude.

YOU HAVE HEALING POWERS TO CREATE CHANGE

THE HUMAN MIND IS LIKE A magnet. We attract whatever we focus on. To heal, you must be focused. Your thoughts, mind, body, image, soul, and spirit are all endowed with supernatural healing powers for positive change in much the same way that the optic nerves power the eyes for vision, the auditory nerves power the ears to enhance hearing, and the sciatic nerves power the muscles of the legs to enhance locomotion. You need not understand the physiology behind this premise. You only need to feel these innate and healing powers located inside you, listen with rapt attention when your inner voice speaks, and then act with faith to see the answers within you, shining as bright as the daytime sun.

If you're sick but focus only on good health, the attractive forces of your mind will magnetize good health by aligning with the medical discoveries, equipment, professionals, and good energies around you to heal you. Focus enhances creativity. Focus, action, and prayer produce unbelievable things. These are called miracles. If you focus on healing, you receive healing; if you focus on illness, you may end up a hypochondriac. If you focus on good health, you receive good health. But for this to happen, you must be dynamic, evolving with a vision and never giving up. You must be resilient. Resilience means clinging tightly to your vision without yielding to any intrinsic or extrinsic force.

To navigate life, you must develop a bounce-back mentality. If you hang on with faith, you'll see the light of day and all the answers needed to create healing. What do you do with the answers? Work on them. Align your movement to the direction of universal flow. Give thanks as you navigate the multitude of changes that life brings to you. Change, an inevitable part of life, is a blessing, it makes you wiser, tougher, and more grounded. It is a rare privilege to feel and accept change. A progressive life requires embracing and appreciating change. When you do, people will react, feel the change, and partner with you to further your cause. So brace up, eschew mediocrity, stay positive, harness your healing powers, get excited about life, and make that change. Stop worrying about things you cannot change right now, rather be patient. Cancel all the pity parties, and schedule appreciation and thanksgiving parties. Harness your innate potential and the golden opportunities God gives you, and fine-tune them into beautiful projects.

There is a divine call inspiring you to stop being a loser. Losers are weak chickens. They disappear when the going gets tough. When the disciples of progressive change call upon them to stand assume confidence and get to work, they pull back, chicken out, and sit at home watching television and making peanut butter and jelly sandwiches and ice tea. Sounds funny, right? But as a champion and a disciple for positive change, you join the other positive people who have been called upon, learn from their wealth of knowledge, study their game and their character, and mimic their movement. Immerse yourself in their circle, and create a mental image of your desires. Stop idling around, stay away from useless people who distract you, and never let their useless drama, negativity, stupidity, or chicken mentality influence your drive to creativity.

Associate more with people who add to your life. Stand out because you were created to do so. You're an achiever, so tap into your innate resources to affect the world. You have divine energy to create positive change, and once you create such change, acknowledge, celebrate, and enjoy every victory because these victories constitute the accelerating force needed to motivate you. Constantly follow directives from the gifts within to fine-tune your acts. We all have gifts. Everyone is blessed with at least five gifts. Place your right hand on your forehead and declare, "I have great gifts inside me." Now activate those gifts, by defining what area your passion resonates with and develop it further then use those gifts to enhance your life. Your cell phone requires activation to work. Your bank card must be activated for you to make purchases. The same applies to your gifts. Simply existing, they are useless, but once they are activated, they have great potency. Gifts are like gold. The more they are refined, the more they shine. Treat your gifts like gold, and you'll be amazed by the results.

Why were you born here and not on Mars, Neptune, or Jupiter? The answer is simple: your services are needed here. God deposited a seed inside you at conception that must be nurtured, harvested, and released in order to affect the world. When the apostle Paul harvested and released his seed while in prison in Babylon, he exploded with fame and etched his name in the annals of history. When Oprah Winfrey harvested seeds on the inside despite all the challenges she faced growing up, she metamorphosed into a world celebrity. When the late Nelson Mandela harvested his divine gifts, he became a global phenomenon and etched his name in gold. When Eddie Murphy put his seed to good use, he became a great force in movie making. Likewise the late Michael Jackson nurtured his seed and became a world superstar at a very tender age, later transforming into a ferocious force in the entertainment industry. The reason these great people leaped to heights that inspire the world today is the same: they nurtured and released their seed.

Every human seed is unique. What are you good at? What seeds are unique to your personality, and how are you nurturing them? Search and you'll discover, and when you do, release your seed to the world with faith. Understand that faith is not mathematics, not calculus, not algebra or permutations. It is a two-word formula—have faith— and is not as complicated as industrial chemistry. But in order to feel the power of faith, you must believe in its existence. If you speak, live, and act faith, it will take over your life to favor you. Then you can create an amazing life that'll take you to places you never dreamed of.

In order to receive, you must be willing to accept the various blessings that God has in store for you. You must be in an attitude of expectancy with a receptive spirit. This is the way it works. When someone gives you a compliment like "You look very beautiful," I like your tie," I like your shoes," or "Your smiles are just cute," you must accept that small gift with gratitude that someone cares. Do you receive compliments with humility in your heart, or do you shut down your appreciation channel and walk away with a tight face? To attract abundance, you must accept the little things that the universe presents to you. That's how the law of abundance works. Change your abundance channel today and activate your gratitude frequency to open doors for the abundance the universe has for you.

POWER CORNER

You have great innate healing powers in you capable of creating change. Ignite and put them to good use today. You'll be amazed on how far you'll go. Remember you have The 9 Power Principles for Change right inside you.

FORTY-FIVE POWER QUOTES FOR POSITIVE CHANGE

1. If you believe in yourself and trust your instincts, you can achieve anything you set your mind to.

2. Determination means you're working very hard with focus to make a change.

3. Faith assures us that if we ask and believe with assurance, we will receive.

4. Every human being has the power to excel, including you.

5. Your chances of succeeding have a lot to do with your mentality.

6. You never know what powers you possess until you start taking powerful actions.

7. Believe in yourself, work hard, make positive moves and you'll sure achieve.

8. Every success story is a product of hard work, perseverance, faith, and God's touch.

9. Challenges are only but temporary. Hang on, stay in faith, and you'll overcome.

10. If you're doing something today, you're investing something in tomorrow.

11. Gratitude means being thankful even for the smallest blessings you receive.

12. Be confident, and never let anyone intimidate or shortchange your talent.

13. Don't let a negative attitude deny you of your free right of gratitude.

14. Dream and act on your dreams. You'll be amazed by what you achieve.

15. If your mental energy is negative, change it to positive. It'll benefit you.

16. When the road gets tough, you must toughen up to face the challenges.

17. Never let your dreams die. If you fail, get up and dream again.

18. Do something today to invest something in your tomorrow.

19. If you ask, declare, believe, and work with faith without giving up, you'll make it happen.

20. Every positive thing you do is a step toward creating a great life for yourself.

21. There is no cap to your achievement potential. Step up your game today.

22. Believe in yourself and never let anyone make you feel second class.

23. There are golden opportunities everywhere. Seek, find, and utilize them.

24. Connect to people with positive energy, and tap from their positivity.

25. You can achieve anything you believe in. Believe in your dreams.

26. Results are for those who finish. Work to fruition. You never know how it'll change you.

27. Everyone has powerful innate gifts. Put yours to good use today.

28. Boost your drive for success. You'll be creating avenues for greatness.

29. Hang around people who motivate you, and tap from their positive energy.

30. Giving opens doors of blessings for you. Give something today.

31. The more successful you are, the more you should be a blessing to others.

32. Bless others constantly—not only when they sneeze. You'll be blessed back.

33. Every dream is big and has great potential. Act. Live your dream today.

34. Do nothing, achieve nothing. Do something, achieve something.

35. Possess an attitude of gratitude at all times. It's the right thing to do.

36. Negativity slows your progress. Think positive and move faster.

37. Little things done with focus and gratitude become steps to increase your altitude.

38. Believe. Live your dream. You're the only one holding yourself back.

39. Giving opens great doors for blessings. Don't be stingy; give and give.

40. Perseverance is a sign that if you don't give up, you'll achieve.

41. When people don't understand your modus operandi, they give you strange names.

42. Don't ever let negative criticism distract you from your focus to achieve.

43. If everyone around you is happy, you're not creating big things.

44. When there is action, people react positively by supporting or negatively by disorganizing. Be wary.

45. You are endowed with innate resources to achieve great things. Step up your game today, keep moving forward, I am rooting for you.

ONE LAST PIECE OF INSPIRATION.

When we connect, align forces, and join our minds, we slough off mediocrity, banish negativity, introduce positivity, enforce a dynamic movement, and change our thinking and our lives. Then we create unimaginable things.

ABOUT THE AUTHOR

Azuka Zuke is a disciple of the movement for positive change.

Born in a small village in Eastern Nigeria, West Africa, he grew up under the tutelage of very strict disciplinarian parents. He went to school five days a week, often barefoot. On Saturdays he accompanied his mom to the farm to cultivate various products. Each new week began with a Sunday mass at church. Faced with the trials inherent in third-world countries, he learned to thrive on two meals a day. Azuka graduated from high school, which was near impossible with tuition funds being so scarce, and then attained a university education—another big hurdle. Finally the green light came on, and he immigrated to America.

Looking through the tiny airplane window to catch a glimpse of the Western world, thousands of miles above sea level, Azuka caught a glimpse of the Statue of Liberty as his flight from Holland approached New York. There was a smile on his face and joy in his heart. He remembers touching down at the airport as one of the greatest joys his life has brought. He cleared customs and continued his onward journey, looking through the windows of the car while appreciating the beautiful view of the American nation.

Azuka settled down to begin a brand-new life in America, God's own country. He found himself dazed and amazed by the beauty of America—the nice roads, the healthy trees lining the streets, the diversity of people, the food. Then, like every other person, Azuka began the race. Starting life anew was a challenge. He worked a couple of jobs to get by to fit into the system and cleared a couple of hurdles, all in the name of living the dream.

Now settled and giving thanks for America, he is realizing the dream bit by bit, meeting new people, and has made a career of engaging and empowering the masses while creating positive movements. First with The Power to Excel and now with The 9 Power Principles for Change, Azuka continues to create a positive force in this beautiful land while appreciating the difference from his motherland, Nigeria, a blessed nation in West Africa.

CONNECT WITH THE AUTHOR

Azuka Zuke Obi, author of The 9 Power Principles for Change, can be reached using the following mediums. You have his noble assurance that he'll get back to you for discussion, comments, and feedback. You can also join his mailing list; rest assured that your e-mail address will be kept private.

E-mail: azukazuke@gmail.com

E-mail: caloburnfit@gmail.com

Facebook: facebook.com/Author Zuke Azuka

Twitter: @zubby34

Website: www.AzukaZuke.com

(A Movement for Positive Change)

MOTIVATIONAL SPEAKING

Azuka Zuke, also called Mr. Inspiration, strongly believes that humans are capable of achieving great things if they are constantly inspired. He is a motivator and continues to be a force in empowerment while imparting wisdom, confidence, and power. To have him appear live or speak at your next event, e-mail azukazuke@gmail.com.

For audios, books, inspiration, motivation, and upcoming speaking events, please visit his website: **www.AzukaZuke.com**.

APPRECIATING YOU

Thank you for reading my book. I pray you found very useful information for your personal development. I will be very grateful if you could post your honest reviews at Amazon.com and on other sites where this book is sold, or e-mail me a blurb or testimonial for marketing.

Thank you a billion times in advance and may the power of change always be with you.

ALSO BY THE AUTHOR

Check out The Power to Excel: Reaching for Your Best, a self-help book that I also authored. This self-development book teaches readers how to use innate resources to achieve success. In The Power to Excel, readers will discover motivation, strength, inspiration, and feel empowered to make positive changes in their lives.

Kirkus Reviews described the book as *"a debut self-help guide that aims to put the power of change in the reader's hands."*

"A motivational guide to improving one's life through changing one's mind-set."

Foreword Reviews/Clarion Review, asserts, *"Like a long and somewhat drawn out conversation with a friend, Obi passes along secrets of success gained while traveling the world and experiencing different cultures and values"* and concludes *"the book guides readers through common themes including snippets on the laws of attraction, the power of positive thinking, visualization, diet, fitness, sleep, charity, faith, friendship and service."*

The book is currently available on Amazon.com as a paperback, on Kindle as an e-book, on Audible.com and iTunes as an audiobook, and in various online bookstores and retailers including BN.com and Books-A-Million.com.

ISBN Paperback: 978-0-61570-644-3

ISBN eBook: 978-1-63001-200-7

Made in the USA
Middletown, DE
11 February 2015